CAMBRIDGE LIBRARY COLLECTION

Books of enduring scholarly value

Anthropology

The first use of the word 'anthropology' in English was recorded in 1593, but its modern use to indicate the study and science of humanity became current in the late nineteenth century. At that time a separate discipline had begun to evolve from many component strands (including history, archaeology, linguistics, biology and anatomy), and the study of so-called 'primitive' peoples was given impetus not only by the reports of individual explorers but also by the need of colonial powers to define and classify the unfamiliar populations which they governed. From the ethnographic writings of early explorers to the 1898 Cambridge expedition to the Torres Straits, often regarded as the first truly 'anthropological' field research, these books provide eye-witness information on often vanished peoples and ways of life, as well as evidence for the development of a new scientific discipline.

The Right Hand: Left-Handedness

Throughout history, left-handedness has been viewed as being the mark of the devil, as evidence of mental retardation or neurosis, as showing a predisposition to criminality, or as being linked to every perceived social ill. Even into the nineteenth century, many scientists were of the opinion that left-handedness was the sign of a sinister personality. An eminent ethnologist and one of the first scientific archaeologists, Daniel Wilson (1816–92), who introduced into English the word 'prehistoric', became aware of the fact that there were as many left-handed Stone Age implements as right. As a left-hander himself, he was fascinated by these discoveries. Published in 1891, his last major work gives the results of his studies of left-handedness, which he concludes is hereditary and relates to the dominance of one hemisphere of the brain.

Cambridge University Press has long been a pioneer in the reissuing of out-of-print titles from its own backlist, producing digital reprints of books that are still sought after by scholars and students but could not be reprinted economically using traditional technology. The Cambridge Library Collection extends this activity to a wider range of books which are still of importance to researchers and professionals, either for the source material they contain, or as landmarks in the history of their academic discipline.

Drawing from the world-renowned collections in the Cambridge University Library and other partner libraries, and guided by the advice of experts in each subject area, Cambridge University Press is using state-of-the-art scanning machines in its own Printing House to capture the content of each book selected for inclusion. The files are processed to give a consistently clear, crisp image, and the books finished to the high quality standard for which the Press is recognised around the world. The latest print-on-demand technology ensures that the books will remain available indefinitely, and that orders for single or multiple copies can quickly be supplied.

The Cambridge Library Collection brings back to life books of enduring scholarly value (including out-of-copyright works originally issued by other publishers) across a wide range of disciplines in the humanities and social sciences and in science and technology.

The Right Hand: Left-Handedness

DANIEL WILSON

CAMBRIDGE
UNIVERSITY PRESS

CAMBRIDGE UNIVERSITY PRESS

Cambridge, New York, Melbourne, Madrid, Cape Town,
Singapore, São Paolo, Delhi, Mexico City

Published in the United States of America by Cambridge University Press, New York

www.cambridge.org
Information on this title: www.cambridge.org/9781108053068

© in this compilation Cambridge University Press 2012

This edition first published 1891
This digitally printed version 2012

ISBN 978-1-108-05306-8 Paperback

THE RIGHT HAND:

LEFT-HANDEDNESS

NATURE SERIES

THE RIGHT HAND:
LEFT-HANDEDNESS

BY

SIR DANIEL WILSON, LL.D., F.R.S.E.

PRESIDENT OF THE UNIVERSITY OF TORONTO
AUTHOR OF 'THE PREHISTORIC ANNALS OF SCOTLAND'
'PREHISTORIC MAN: RESEARCHES INTO THE
ORIGIN OF CIVILISATION,' ETC.

London

MACMILLAN AND CO.

AND NEW YORK

1891

TO

HIS GRANDSON

OSWALD GEORGE WILSON BELL

THIS LITTLE VOLUME

IS AFFECTIONATELY DEDICATED

BY

THE AUTHOR

PREFACE

THE following treatise includes data originally
accumulated in a series of papers communicated to the Canadian Institute and the Royal
Society of Canada, aiming at determining the
cause of Left-handedness by a review of its
history in its archæological, philological, and
physiological aspects. In revising the materials
thus accumulated in illustration of the subject,
with a view to their publication in a connected
form, the results of later investigation have
been embodied here, not only with the aim of
tracing Left-handedness to its true source,
and thereby proving the folly of persistently

striving to suppress an innate faculty of exceptional aptitude, but also to enforce the advantages to be derived by all from a systematic cultivation of dexterity in both hands.

BENCOSIE, TORONTO,
24th April 1891.

CONTENTS

CHAPTER VII

CHAPTER VIII

CHAPTER IX

CHAPTER X

CHAPTER XI

CHAPTER I

THE HAND

THE hand is one of the most distinctive character-
istics of man. Without its special organisation
he would be for all practical purposes inferior
to many other animals. It is the executive portion of the upper limb whereby the limits of
his capacity as "the tool-user" are determined.
As such, it is the active agent of the primary
sense of touch, the organ of the will, the instrument which works harmoniously with brain
and heart, and by means of which imagination
and idealism are translated into fact. Without it man's intellectual superiority would be
to a large extent abortive. In its combina-
tion of strength with delicacy, it is an index of
character in all its variations in man and woman

from childhood to old age. It is an exponent of the refinement of high civilisation, no less than the organ of all dexterity and force of the skilled inventor and mechanician. In the art of the true painter, as in works of Titian and Vandyke, the portraiture of the hand is no less replete with individuality than the face.

In so far as the hand is to be recognised as the organ of touch or feeling, it plays a different part from the other organs of the senses. It is no mere passive recipient of impressions, but selects the objects to be subjected to its discrimination, and communicates the results to the central organ: the seat of intelligence. As a responsive agent of the mind it is the productive artificer. In its independent estimate of form and texture it performs for all of us the function of sight in the darkness; and to the blind it is an eye wherewith they are enabled to receive correct impressions of external nature, and to read for themselves the lettered page. The hand, moreover, has an utterance of its own. The unpremeditated actions of the orator harmoniously emphasise his speech; and in strong emotional excitement, the movements of the hands are scarcely less expressive than the tongue. There are, indeed,

occasions when its symbolic speech needs no audible
accompaniment. The repelling action of the out-
stretched palm, accompanied by the averted head,
can dispense with words; and the hand in benediction has no need of them. The imagination realises
the amplest significance of such gestures, as in the
final parting of Arthur and Guinevere—

> She in the darkness o'er her fallen head
> Perceived the waving of his hands that blest.

In discussing the specialty of right-handedness,
either as an expansion or limitation of the use of
the hand, it is not necessary to enlarge on the
distinctive anatomical relations of the human hand
to the fore-limb of other animals; for if the final
results here set forth are correct, the preferential
and instinctive employment of one limb and extremity is not an exclusive attribute of man
Nevertheless the hand is one of the most characteristic human features. The practical distinction
between man and any approximate living creature
lies in the fact that the most highly developed
anthropoid, while in a sense four-handed, has no
such delicate instrument of manipulation as that
which distinguishes man from all other animals.
In most monkeys there is a separate and movable

thumb in all the four limbs. The characteristic whereby their hallux, or great toe, instead of being parallel with the others, and so adapted for standing and walking erect, has the power of action of a thumb, gives the prehensile character of a hand to the hind-limb. This is not confined to the arboreal apes. It is found in the baboons and others that are mainly terrestrial in their habits, and employ the four limbs ordinarily in moving on the ground.

The human hand is an organ so delicately fashioned that the biologist has, not unnaturally, turned to it in search of a typical structural significance. By reason of its mobility and its articulated structure, it is specially adapted to be an organ of touch ; and the fine sense which education confers on it tends still further to widen the difference between the human hand and that of the ape. Hence Cuvier's long-accepted determination of a separate order for man as bimanous. But this classification is no longer tenable. Man is, indeed, still admitted to form a single genus, *Homo* ; but in the levelling process of scientific revolution he has been relegated to a place in the same order with the monkeys and, possibly, the lemurs, which in the development of the thumb

are more manlike than the apes. In reality,
looking simply to man as thus compared with the
highest anthropoid apes, the order of Quadrumana
is more open to challenge than that of the Bimana.
The hind-limb of the ape approaches anatomically
much more to the human foot than the hand;
while the fore-limb is a true though inferior hand.
The ape's hind-limb is indeed prehensile, as is the
foot of man in some degree; but alike anatomically
and physiologically the fore-limb of the ape, like
the hand of man, is the prehensile organ *par
excellence*; while the primary function of the hind-
limb is locomotion.

There are unquestionably traces of prehensile
capacity in the human foot; and even of remarkable adaptability to certain functions of the hand.
Well-known cases have occurred of persons born
without hands, or early deprived of them, learning
to use their feet in many delicate operations,
including not only the employment of pen and
pencil, but the use of scissors, with a facility which
demonstrates the latent capacity for separate action
of the great toe, and its thumblike apposition to
the others. In 1882 I witnessed, in the Museum
at Antwerp, an artist without arms skilfully use

his brushes with his right foot. He employed it
with great ease, arranging his materials, opening
his box of colours, selecting and compressing his
tubes, and "handling" his brush, seemingly with
a dexterity fully equal to that of his more favoured
rivals. At an earlier date, during a visit to Boston,
I had an opportunity of observing a woman, under
similar disadvantages, execute elaborate pieces of
scissor-work, and write not only with neatness, but
with great rapidity. Nevertheless the human foot,
in its perfect natural development, is not a hand.
The small size of the toes as compared with the
fingers, and the position and movements of the great
toe, alike point to diverse functions and a greatly
more limited range of action. But the capacity of
the system of muscles of the foot — scarcely less
elaborate than that of the hand,—is obscured to us
by the rigid restraints of the modern shoe. The
power of voluntary action in the toes manifests
itself not only in cases where early mutilation, or
malformation at birth, compels the substitution of
the foot for the hand; but among savages, where
the unshackled foot is in constant use in climbing
and feeling its way through brake and jungle, the
free use of the toes, and the power of separating

the great toe from the others, are retained in the
same way as may be seen in the involuntary
movements of a healthy child.   When camping
out in long vacation holidays in the Canadian
wilds, repeated experience has proved to me that
the substitution for a few weeks of the soft, yield-
ing deerskin moccasin of the Indian, in place of the
rigid shoe, restores even to the unpractised foot of
civilised man a freedom of action in the toes, a
discriminating sense of touch, and a capacity for
grasping rock or tree in walking or climbing, of
which he has had no previous conception.   The
Australian picks up his spear with the naked foot;
and the moccasin of the American Indian scarcely
diminishes the like capacity to take hold of stick or
stone.   The Hindu tailor, in like manner, sits on
the ground holding the cloth tightly stretched with
his toes, while both hands are engaged in the work
of the needle.

Such facts justify the biologist in regarding this
element of structural difference between man and
the apes as inadequate for the determination of a
specific zoological classification.   Nevertheless man
still stands apart as the tool-maker, the tool-user,
the manipulator.   A comparison between the fore

and hind limbs of the Chimpanzee, or other ape, leaves the observer in doubt whether to name them alike as hands or feet, both being locomotive as well as prehensile organs; whereas the difference between the hand and foot of man is obvious, and points to essentially diverse functions. The short, weak thumb, the long, nearly uniform fingers, and the inferior play of the wrist in the monkey, are in no degree to be regarded as defects. They are advantageous to the tree-climber, and pertain to its hand as an organ of locomotion; whereas the absence of such qualities in the human hand secures its permanent delicacy of touch, and its general adaptation for many manipulative purposes.

The hand of man is thus eminently adapted to be the instrument for translating the conceptions of intelligent volition into concrete results. Dr. George Wilson in his fine prose poem : " The Five Gateways of Knowledge," speaks of it as giving expression " to the genius and the wit, the courage and the affection, the will and the power of man. . . . The term handicraftsman or hand-worker belongs to all honest, earnest men and women, and is a title which each should covet. For the Queen's hand there is the sceptre, and for the soldier's hand the sword ; for the carpenter's hand the saw, and for the smith's hand the hammer; for the farmer's hand the plough, for the miner's hand the spade, for the sailor's hand the oar, for the painter's hand the brush, for the sculptor's hand the chisel, for the poet's hand the pen, and for the woman's hand the needle. If none of these, or the like, will fit us, the felon's chain should be round our wrist, and our hand on the prisoner's crank. But for each willing man and woman there is a tool they may learn to handle; for all there is the command : ' Whatsoever thy hand findeth to do, do it with all thy might.' "

Other animals have their implements for constructive skill, and their weapons, offensive and defensive, as parts of their organic being; and are armed, equipped, clad, and mailed by no effort of their own. But man, inferior to all in offensive and defensive appliances, is a match for his most formidable assailants by means of appliances furnished by his dexterous hand in obedience to the promptings of intelligent volition.

The matured capacity of the hand is the necessary concomitant of man's intellectual development; not only enabling him to fashion all needful tools, and to place at a disadvantage the fiercest of his assailants

armed by nature with formidable weapons of assault ;
but also to respond no less effectually to every
prompting of the æsthetic faculty in the most delicate
artistic creations.   The very arts of the ingenious
nest-makers, the instinctive weavers or builders, the
spider, the bee, the ant, or the beaver, place them in
striking contrast to man in relation to his handiwork.
He alone, in the strict sense of the term, is a
manufacturer.   The Quadrumana, though next to
man in the approximation of their fore-limbs to
hands, claim no place among the instinctive
architects, weavers, or spinners.   The human hand,
as an instrument of constructive design or artistic
skill, ranks wholly apart from all the organs
employed in the production of analogous work
among the lower animals.   The hand of the ape
accomplishes nothing akin to the masonry of the
swallow, or the damming and building of the
beaver.   But, imperfect though it seems, it suffices
for all requirements of the forest-dweller.   In
climbing trees, in gathering and shelling nuts or
pods, opening shell-fish, tearing off the rind of fruit,
or pulling up roots ; in picking out thorns or burs
from its own fur, or in the favourite occupation
of hunting for each other's parasites : the monkey

uses the finger and thumb; and in many other operations performs with the hand what is executed by the quadruped or bird less effectually by means of the mouth or bill. At first sight we might be tempted to assume that the quadrumanous mammal had the advantage of us, as there are certainly many occasions when an extra hand could be turned to useful account. But not only do man's two hands prove greatly more serviceable for all higher purposes of manipulation than the four hands of the ape: a further specialty distinguishing him as he rises in the scale of intellectual superiority is that he seems to widen still more the divergence from the quadrumanous anthropoid by converting one hand into the favoured organ and servant of his will, while the other is relegated to a wholly subordinate place as its mere help and supplement.

CHAPTER II

THE EDUCATED HAND

THE reign of law is a phrase comprehensive enough
to embrace many points of minor import; and
among those assigned to its sway the prevalent
habit of right-handedness has been recognised as
one of too familiar experience to seem to stand in
need of further explanation. It has been accepted
as the normal usage and law of action common to
the whole race; and so no more in need of any
special reason for its existence than any other
function of the hand. Nevertheless it has not
wholly eluded investigation; nor is it surprising
that the exceptional but strongly marked deviations
from the normal law should have attracted the
notice of thoughtful observers to the question of
right-handedness as a curious and unsolved problem.

A philosophic speculator of the seventeenth century, the famous old Norwich physician, Sir Thomas Browne, reverts characteristically to the mystic fancies of the Talmud for guidance, as he turns to the question in its simplest aspect, and quaintly ignores the existence of its foundation. With his strong bent towards Platonic mysticism, this question, like other and higher speculations with which he dallied, presented itself in relation to what may well be called "first principles," as an undetermined problem. "Whether," says he in his *Religio Medici*, "Eve was framed out of the left side of Adam, I dispute not, because I stand not yet assured which is the right side of a man, or whether there be any such distinction in nature." That there is a right side in man is a postulate not likely to be seriously disputed; but whether there is such a distinction in nature remains still unsettled two centuries and a half after the inquiry was thus started. The same question was forced on the attention of an eminent philosophic speculator of our own day, under circumstances that involved a practical realisation of its significance. Towards the close of a long life in which Thomas Carlyle had unceasingly plied his busy pen, the dexterous right hand, that had un-

flaggingly toiled for upwards of threescore years in
the service of his fellow-men, was suddenly paralysed.
The period of life was all too late for him to turn
with any hope of success to the unaccustomed and
untrained left hand; and more than one entry in
his journal refers to the irreparable loss.   But one
curious embodiment of the reflections suggested by
this privation is thus recorded by him upwards of a
year after experience had familiarised him with all
that the loss involved: " Curious to consider the
institution of the Right hand among universal mankind; probably the very oldest human institution
that exists, indispensable to all human co-operation
whatsoever.   He that has seen three mowers, one
of whom is left-handed, trying to work together,
and how impossible it is, has witnessed the simplest
form of an impossibility, which but for the distinction of a 'right hand,' would have pervaded all
human things.   Have often thought of all that,
—never saw it so clearly as this morning while out
walking, unslept and dreary enough in the windy
sunshine.   How old?   Old!   I wonder if there is
any people barbarous enough not to have this distinction of hands; no human Cosmos possible to be
even begun without it.   Oldest Hebrews, etc., writ-

ing from right to left, are as familiar with the world-
old institution as we. Why that particular hand
was chosen is a question not to be settled, not
worth asking except as a kind of riddle; probably
arose in fighting; most important to protect your
heart and its adjacencies, and to carry the shield on
that hand."

This idea of the left hand being preoccupied
with the shield, and so leaving to the other the
active functions of the sword and spear hand, is
familiar to the classical student, and will fitly come
under review at a later stage. Nor can such
secondary influences be overlooked. Whatever may
prove to be the primary source of right-handedness,
it cannot be doubted that, when thoroughly developed and systematically recognised as determining
the character of many combined operations, the
tendency would inevitably be to foster the preferential use of the right hand even in indifferent actions.
Two causes have thus to be recognised as operating
in the development of right-handedness, and begetting certain differences in its manifestation under
varying social influences. There is a progressive
scale, from the imperfect to the more perfectly
developed, and then to the perfectly educated hand :

all steps in its adaptation to the higher purposes of the manipulator. The hand of the rude savage, of the sailor, the miner, or blacksmith, while well fitted for the work to which it is applied, is a very different instrument from that of the chaser, engraver, or cameo-cutter; of the musician, painter, or sculptor. This difference is unquestionably a result of development, whatever the other may be; for, as we have in the ascending scale the civilised and educated man, so also we have the educated hand as one of the most characteristic features of civilisation. But here attention is at once called to the distinctive preference of the right hand, whether as the natural use of this more perfect organ of manipulation, or as an acquired result of civilisation. The phenomenon to be explained is not merely why each individual uses one hand rather than another. Experience abundantly accounts for this. But if it can be shown that all nations, civilised and savage, appear to have used the same hand, it is vain to look for the origin of this as an acquired habit. Only by referring it to some anatomical cause can its general prevalence, among all races and in every age, be satisfactorily accounted for. Nevertheless this simple pheno-

menon, cognisant to the experience of all, and
brought under constant notice in our daily inter-
course with others, long baffled the physiologist in
his search for a satisfactory explanation.

The sense of touch—"The Feel-Gate" of Bun-
yan's famous Town of Mansoul,—is not limited,
like the other senses, to one special organ, but
pervades the entire body; and in its acute susceptibility to every irritant contact, communicates in-
stantaneously with the vital cerebral centre of the
whole nervous system by means of the electric chords
or nerves. So effectual is this that "if one member
suffer, all the members suffer with it." Nevertheless
the hand is correctly recognised as the active organ
of feeling; and by the delicately sensitive and well-
trained fingers impressions are promptly conveyed
to the brain and to the mind, relative to the
qualities of all bodies within reach of the unfailing
test of touch. In hearing and seeing the dual
organs are in constant co-operation, and the injury
of either involves a loss of power. But though we
have two hands sensitive to all external impressions,
only one of them is habitually recognised as the
active agent of the brain; and except in a comparatively small number of cases, this is the hand on

the right side of the body. It is surprising that this phenomenon so universally recognised as what may be styled an instinctive attribute of man, should not long since have been traced to its true source. Yet, as will be seen, some among the ablest anatomists have been content to refer it to mere habit, stereotyped by long usage and the exigencies of combined action into a general practice; while others have referred it to the disposition of the viscera, and the place of the heart on the left side.

The hand is the universal symbol of amity; at once the organ and the emblem of friendly co-operation and brotherhood. The mystic grip of the freemason is older than the builder's art. In the gesture-language so largely in use among savage tribes the hands take the place of the tongue; and the relations of the right and left hand acquire fresh significance in the modification of signs. Mr. Garrick Mallery gives the expression of amity among the Otos thus: "The left and right hands are brought to centre of the chest open, then extended, and the left hand, with palm up, is grasped crosswise by right hand with palm down, and held thus." So in like manner among the Dakotas: "The left hand held horizontal, palm inward, fingers and thumb extended

SYMBOLIC MONOGRAPH, MORO INSCRIBED ROCK,
RIO DE ZUÑI.

To face page 19.

and pointing towards the right, is clasped by the right hand." In those and other expressive gestures the left hand is employed to indicate the *non ego* : the other than the gesture-maker.

So also among other rude Indian tribes of North America, no less than among the civilised and lettered nations in the centres of native civilisation in Mexico, Central America, and Peru, the hand is familiarly employed not only as a graven or written symbol, but is literally impressed, apparently as the equivalent of a signet. The sign of the expanded right hand touching the left arm occupies a prominent place among the graven hieroglyphics on an Aztec stone hatchet shown by Humboldt in his *Vues des Cordilleres*. The graven Moro Rock in the valley of the Rio de Zuñi includes more than one similar device among its elaborate inscriptions and pictographs ; one of which is specially noticeable. Inscriptions in the Spanish language, some of them with dates referable to the first intrusion of European explorers, are intermingled with the native hieroglyphs. In one example the sacred monograph I.H.S. is enclosed in the same cartouch with an open hand characterised by a double thumb,—possibly the native counterpart to the Christian symbol,—a hand of superhuman capacity and power. School-craft says : " The figure of the human hand is used by the North American Indians to denote supplica-tion to the Deity or Great Spirit ; and it stands in the system of picture-writing as the symbol for strength, power, or mastery thus derived." But the use of the hand as the chief organ of gesture-language shows how varied are the applications that it admits of as a significant emblem. Washington Irving remarks in his *Astoria* : " The Arickaree warriors were painted in the most savage style. Some had the stamp of a red hand across their mouths, a sign that they had drunk the life-blood of a foe." Catlin found the same symbol in use not only for decoration, but as the actual sign-manual among the Omahaws and the Mandans. I have repeatedly observed the red hand impressed on the buffalo robe, and also occasionally on the naked breast of the Chippewas of Lake Superior.

In the sculptured hieroglyphics of Central America, and in the Mexican picture-writings, the human and other profiles are introduced in the large majority of examples looking to the left, as would be the natural result of the tracings of a right-handed draftsman. But the hand is also

employed symbolically; while, among the civilised
Peruvians, the impress of the naked hand was
practised in the same way as by the Indians of the
northern continent. Among an interesting collection of mummies recovered by Mr. J. H. Blake of
Boston from ancient Peruvian cemeteries on the
Bay of Chacota, one is the body of a female wrapped
in parti-coloured garments of fine texture, and
marked on the outer woollen wrappings with the
impress of a human hand. The same impress of
the red hand is common on Peruvian mummies.

The hand or the thumb as a signet possesses a
specific individuality. The lines on the surface of
the thumb, as also on the finger-tips, form a definite
pattern; and there is some reason for believing
that it is perpetuated, with slight modifications, as
an element of heredity. But apart from this, the
individual hand is replete with character when
carefully studied; and the impress of the native
hand on dress and buildings attracted the notice of
Stephens in his exploration of the antiquities of
Central America. The skulls and complete mummies
recovered from Peruvian tombs show them to pertain to a small race; and the impress of the little
hand made on the mummies with red pigment

recalls the *mano-colorado* described by Stephens as a common feature amid the ruins of Uxmall: the impression of a living hand, but so small that it was completely hid under that of the traveller or his companion.   It afterwards stared them in the face, as he says, on all the ruined buildings of the country; and on visiting a nameless ruin beyond Sabachtsche, in Yucatan, Stephens remarks: " On the walls of the desolate edifice were prints of the *mano-colorado,* or red hand.   Often as I saw this print, it never failed to interest me.   It was the stamp of the living hand.   It always brought me nearer to the builders of these cities ; and at times, amid stillness, desolation, and ruin, it seemed as if from behind the curtain that concealed them from view was extended the hand of greeting.   The Indians said it was the hand of the master of the building."

CHAPTER III

THE WILLING HAND

THE human hand is not only the symbol of the intelligent artificer, " the hand of the master," the sign and epitome of the lord and ruler; it is the instrument of the will alike for good and evil deeds. The idea of it as the active participator in every act embodies itself in all vocabularies. The imperial mandate, the lordly manumission, the skilled manufacturer, the handy tool, the unhandy workman, the left-handed stroke, the handless drudge, with other equally familiar terms, all refer to the same ever-ready exponent of the will; so that we scarcely recognise the term as metaphorical when we speak of the " willing hand." The Divine appeal to the wrathful prophet of Nineveh is based on the claim for mercy on behalf of those who had not yet attained to the first stage of dexterity which pertains to childhood. "Should not I spare Nineveh, that great city, wherein are more than sixscore thousand that cannot discern between their right hand and their left?" To this same test of discernment poor Cassio appeals when, betrayed by the malignant craft of Iago, he would fain persuade himself he is not enslaved by the intoxicating draught: "Do not think, gentlemen, I am drunk. This is my right hand, and this is my left!" Only the infant or the drunkard, it is thus assumed, can fail to mark the distinction; and to select the true hand for all honourable service. It is the sceptred hand; the hand to be offered in pledge of amity; the one true wedding hand; the hand of benediction, ordination, consecration; the organ through which human will acts, whether by choice or by organic law. The attempt, therefore, to claim any independent rights or honourable status for the sinister hand seems an act of disloyalty, if not of sacrilege.

But hand and will have co-operated from the beginning in good and in evil; even as in that first erring deed, when Eve—

> Her rash hand, in evil hour
> Forth reaching to the fruit, she pluck'd, she ate;

> Earth felt the wound ; and Nature from her seat
> Sighing through all her works gave signs of woe.

The symbolic and responsible hand accordingly
figures everywhere.   The drama of history and of
fiction are alike full of it.   Pilate vainly washes his
hands as he asserts his innocence of the blood of
the Just One.   "All the perfumes of Arabia will
not sweeten this little hand!" is the agonised cry of
Lady Macbeth.   "This unworthy hand!" exclaims
the martyr, Cranmer, as he makes it expiate the
unfaithful act of signature, as though it were an
independent actor, alone responsible for the deed.
In touching tenderness the venerable poet Longfellow thus symbolised the entrance on life's
experiences—

> Oh, little hands that, weak or strong,
> Have still to rule or serve so long ;
>   Have still so much to give or ask ;
> I, who so long with tongue and pen
> Have toiled among my fellow-men,
>   Am weary thinking of your task.

But childhood speedily reaches the stage when the
privileged hand asserts its prerogative, and assumes
its distinctive responsibility.   For good or evil, not
only does the right hand take precedence in the

established formulæ of speech, but the left hand is
in many languages the symbol or equivalent of im-
purity, degradation, malice, and of evil doings.

Looking then on right-handedness as a very
noticeable human attribute, and one that enters largely
into the daily acts, the exceptional manifestations
of skill, and many habits and usages of life : the
fact is indisputable that, whether we ascribe its
prevalence solely to education, or assign its origin
to some organic difference, the delicacy of the sense
of touch, and the manipulative skill and mobility
of the right hand, in the majority of cases, so far
exceeds that of the left that a term borrowed from
the former expresses the general idea of dexterity.
That education has largely extended the preferential
use of the right hand is undoubted.   That it has
even unduly tended to displace the left hand from
the exercise of its manipulative function, I fully
believe.   But so far as appears, in the preference of
one hand for the execution of many special operations, the choice seems, by general consent, without
any concerted action, to have been that of the right.

The proofs of the antiquity of this consensus
present themselves in ever-increasing amplitude,
leading finally to an investigation of traces appar-

ently showing a prevalent *dexterity* among palæolithic artificers. The paintings and intaglios of ancient Egypt, the sculptures of Nineveh and Babylon, and the later products of Hellenic and Etruscan art, when carefully studied, all yield illustrations of the subject. But the disclosures of archæology in its later co-operation with the researches of the geologist have familiarised us with phases of human history that relegate the builders of the Birs Nimrud, and the sculptors of Nineveh or Thebes, to modern centuries. The handiwork of the palæolithic cave-dwellers and the primitive drift-folk produce to us works of industry and skill, fashioned when art was in its infancy, and metallurgy unknown.

It is unnecessary here to aim at even an approximate estimate of the remoteness of that strange epoch when the cave-dwellers of the Vezere and the northern slopes of the Pyrenees were the contemporaries of the mammoth, the woolly rhinoceros, and the long-extinct carnivora of the caves; and the fossil horse, with the musk-sheep, reindeer, and other Arctic fauna, were objects of the chase among the hunters of the Garonne.

The assignment of the primitive relics of human art to a period when the use of metals was unknown,

and man had to furnish his implements and weapons
solely from such materials as wood, horn, bone, shell,
stone, or flint, has naturally given a novel importance to this class of relics; and we owe to the pen
of Dr. John Evans not only an exhaustive review
of the ancient implements and weapons of Great
Britain, but also, incidentally, of the world's Stone
Age, in nearly all countries and periods. In that
work, accordingly, some of the earliest traces of
man's handiwork, as the manipulator and tool-maker,
are described. Of those the implements of the
River-drift Period are at once the rudest and most
primitive in character. They occur in vast numbers
among the rolled gravel of the ancient fresh water or
river-drifts, of what has received from the included
implements the name of the *Palæolithic Period*; and
if they are correctly assumed to represent the sole
appliances of the man of the Drift Period, they
indicate a singularly rude stage. In reality, however, the large, rude almond and tongue-shaped
implements of flint are nearly imperishable; while
trimmed flakes, small daggers or arrow-heads, and
other delicately fashioned flint implements,—as well
as any made of more perishable materials, such as
shell, wood, or bone,—must have been fractured in

the violence to which the rolled gravels were subjected, or would perish by natural decay.

But the same period is no less definitely illustrated by deposits sealed up through unnumbered
centuries under the stalagmitic flooring of limestone
caves, or in the deposits of river gravels and silt,
filling in many of the caves with red earth and
gravel embedding implements closely resembling
those of the drift. The ossiferous deposits, moreover, found in some of the oldest caves of England,
France, and Belgium, which have disclosed palæolithic tools, include also remains of the mammoth,
cave-bear, fossil-horse, hyæna, reindeer, and other
animals either wholly extinct, or such as prove by
their character the enormous climatic changes referred
to. In so far, therefore, as they afford any indication of the antiquity of man, they point to ages
so remote that it is unnecessary to investigate
the bearings of evidence suggestive of comparative
degrees in time. Every new discovery does, indeed, add to our means of determining a relative
prehistoric chronology which for some aspects of
the inquiry is replete with interest and value.
But the subject is referred to now solely in its
bearing on the subordinate yet significant question

relative to the manipulation of the primitive tool-maker.

Here then, if anywhere, we may hope to find some of the earliest evidences of dexterity, alike in its technical and its popular sense. The primitive Troglodytes of Europe have not only transmitted to us abundant evidence of their industry as tool-makers, but also remarkable illustrations of their imitative art, and of an æsthetic faculty developed into rare excellence under all the disadvantages of the cave-dweller fashioning his own artistic imple-ments in a palæolithic age. In such a stage of social life man was uninfluenced by any necessity for concerted action, and so was free to follow inclination or instinct in the preference for either hand.

CHAPTER IV

ARCHÆOLOGY has undertaken novel duties as the handmaid of history. With its aid we have acquired more definite ideas of the men of Western Europe in its pleistocene or quaternary epoch than we possess of the contemporaries of Greece and Rome in the centuries preceding the Christian era. The huge cave-bear, the cave-lion, with their more formidable congener, the sabre-toothed *Machairodus latidens*, preyed on the mammoth, the woolly rhinoceros, the reindeer, musk-sheep, and other fauna of a semi-arctic climate; and the men of that same epoch, while still ignorant of the very rudiments of metallurgy, fashioned for themselves sufficiently effective weapons to contend successfully with the fiercest of the carnivora, and secure for their own use the

spoils of the chase.   Palæolithic man made his home
in the deserted rock-shelters and caves of the hyæna
and cave-bear; and in spite of the privations of a
rigorous climate, found leisure not only to fashion
his ingenious tools, but to indulge a taste for art,
alike in carving and in etching on ivory and stone,
to an extent altogether remarkable when the whole
attendant circumstances are duly estimated.   Specimens of those primitive works of art, including
ingenious carvings in bone and ivory, and lances,
daggers of deers' horn, maces and batons carved in
bone, and decorated in some cases with artistic skill,
have been recovered from the cave-drift, or more
securely sealed up in the cave-breccia.   The evidences of skill are unmistakable.   Within the last
thirty years repeated discoveries of such ancient
cave-dwellings, and the investigation of their contents, have familiarised us with the workmanship of
their primitive artificers.   The evidence which these
ingenious products furnish in proof of the dexterity
of the ancient cave-men, in the more comprehensive
sense of that term, is universally recognised; but
my attention was first directed to the possible clue
which they might furnish to the prevalent use of
one or other hand in that remote age, by what on

further investigation proved to be an error in the
reproduction of the famous drawing of the mammoth
on a plate of its own ivory, found in La Madelaine
Cave, in the Valley of the Vezere.   In M. Louis
Figuier's *L'Homme Primitif*, for example, which
might be assumed as a reliable authority in reference
to the illustrative examples of French palæolithic
art, the La Madelaine Cave sketch is incorrectly
reproduced as a left-hand drawing ; that is to say, the
mammoth is looking to the right.   This is a nearly
unerring test of right or left-handedness.   The
skilled artist can, no doubt, execute a right or left
profile at his will.   But an unpremeditated profile-
drawing, if done by a right-handed draftsman, will
be represented looking to the left; as, if it is the
work of a left-handed draftsman, it will certainly
look to the right.

The drawings of those contemporaries of the
mammoth and other extinct fauna of Europe have
naturally excited attention on various grounds.
They furnish no uncertain evidence of the intellectual status of the men of that remote age who con-
stituted the population of Southern France, and of
neighbouring regions, under climatic conditions con-
trasting as strangely with those of the sunny land

of the vine and the olive, as did the contemporary
fauna and flora with those of Guyenne or Gascony
at the present day. Any evidence therefore of
their mode of working derived from their carvings
and drawings has a special bearing on an inquiry
into the antiquity and assumed universality of an
instinctive habit.

The examples of primitive art are of varying
degrees of merit. Some of them may be compared
to the first efforts of an untutored youth; while
others, such as the La Madelaine mammoth and the
grazing reindeer from Thayngen, show the practised
hand of a skilled draftsman. Among the fanciful
illustrations introduced by M. Louis Figuier in his
L'Homme Primitif is a picture showing the arts
of drawing and sculpture as practised during the
reindeer epoch. Three men of fine physique, slightly
clad in skins, stand or recline in easy attitudes,
sketching or carving as a modern artist might do in
the lighter hours of his practice. One stands and
sketches a deer, with free hand, on a piece of slate,
which rests against a ledge of rock as his easel.
Another, seated at his ease, traces a miniature device
with, it may be, a pointed flint, on a slab of bone or
ivory. The third is apparently carving or modelling

a deer or other quadruped. All are, as a matter
of course, represented with the stylus, graver, or
modelling tool in the right hand, the question of
possible left-handedness not having occurred to the
modern draftsman.

All experience points to the conclusion that the
primitive artificer habitually used one hand, whether
the right or the left. Even when the naturally
left-handed have acquired such facility in the use of
the right hand, by persevering compliance with the
usage of the majority in many customary practices
of daily life, as to be practically ambidextrous, each
hand is still employed by instinctive preference
in certain definite acts; as with all, the knife is
habitually used in one hand and the fork in the
other. The result never leads to an indiscriminate
employment of either hand. The necessity for
promptness of action in the constantly recurring
operations of daily life is sufficient to superinduce
the habitual employment of one or the other hand
with no more conscious selection than in the
choice of foot, when not under command of a drill
sergeant. Indeed, the experience of many readers,
whose training as volunteers has included that
important branch of education styled " the goose

step," must have convinced them that few questions
are more perplexing to the novice than, " Which is
the right foot, and which is the left ? " In football
no player is in doubt as to the foot he shall use.
In cricket there is no uncertainty as to the choice of
hand for the bat. In digging the action is so certain,
though unpremeditated, that in Ireland, and probably
elsewhere, " the spade-foot " is a term in general use.
It is not necessarily the right foot, but it is always
the same. The unpremeditated action of hand or
foot is uniform, as the reader will find by clasping
his hands with the fingers interlaced, or inviting
another to do so. It is no matter of chance which
thumb shall be uppermost. But combined operations involving close unity of action are rare in
savage life ; and man in the hunter stage is little
affected in his habits by social usage. Hence
spontaneous left-handedness may be looked for more
frequently in such a stage, and even in peasant life,
than in cultured society ; though the occasions for
its manifestation are more rare.

Attention has already been directed to the test
of the diverse direction in which a profile is most
readily, and therefore most naturally, drawn if
executed by the right or the left hand. In so far

as the drawings or etchings of the palæolithic age
are available for the application of this test, the
following data may be adduced :—

The mammoth drawing from La Madelaine Cave;
the bison, imperfect, showing only the hind-
quarters; and the ibex, on reindeer-antler, from
Laugerie Basse; the group of reindeers from the
Dordogne, two walking and one lying on its back;
the cave-bear of the Pyrenees, from the cave of
Massat, in the department of Ariege; and another
sketch representing a hunter stalking the Urus:
may all be regarded as right-hand drawings. But
the horses from La Madelaine, engraved on reindeer-
antler, specially noticeable for their large heads;
the horse, from Creswell Crags; and, above all, the
remarkably spirited drawing of the reindeer grazing,
from Thayngen in the Kesserloch—a sketch, marked
by incident, both in the action of the animal and
its surroundings, suggestive of an actual study from
nature,—all appear to be left-hand drawings.

The number of examples thus far adduced is
obviously too small to admit of any general conclusions as to the relative use of the right or left
hand being based on their evidence; but so far as it
goes, while it presents one striking example of a

left-handed drawing, it confirms the idea of the
predominance of right-handedness at that remote
stage in the history of European man.   It confirms,
moreover, the correctness of the distinction already
made between the preferential use of either hand by
the cultured and skilled workman, or the artist, and
its employment among rude, unskilled labourers engaged in such toil as may be readily accomplished
by either hand.   That the use of the left hand is
transmitted from parent to child, and so, like other
peculiarities, is to some extent hereditary, is undoubted.   This has, therefore, to be kept in view in
drawing any comprehensive deductions from a few
examples confined to two or three localities.   It
may be that the skilled draftsman of the Vézère, or
the gifted artist to whom we owe the Kesserloch
drawing, belonged to a family, or possibly a tribe,
among whom left-handedness prevailed to an unusual extent; and so might be developed not only
hereditarily but by imitation.   But on the other
hand, even among those palæolithic draftsmen, there
is a distinct preference for the right hand in the
majority of cases; and this is just what was to
be expected.   The more the subject is studied it
becomes manifest that education, with the stimulus

furnished by the necessities arising from all combined
action, has much to do with a full development of
right-handedness. The bias is unquestionably in
that direction; but with many it is not so active as to
be beyond the reach of education, such as the habit
and usage of companions would supply, to overcome
it. But with a considerable number the preferential
use of the right hand is prompted by a strong, if
not unconquerable instinctive impulse. A smaller
number are no less strongly impelled to the use of
the left hand. In the ruder conditions of society
each man is free to follow the natural bias; and
in the absence or rare occurrence of the need for
combined action, either habit attracts little attention. But so soon as co-operation begins to
exercise its restraining and constraining influences,
a very slight bias, due probably to individual organic
structure, will suffice to determine the preference
for one hand over the other, and so to originate the
prevalent law of dexterity. The results shown by
the ancient drawings of Europe's cave-men perfectly
accord with this. In that remote dawn every man
did that which was right in his own eyes. Some
handled their tools and drew with the left hand; a
larger number used the right hand; but as yet no

rule prevailed. In this, as in certain other respects, the arts and habits of that period belong to a chapter in the infancy of the race, when the law of dexterity, as well as other laws begot by habit, convenience, or mere prescriptive conventionality, had not yet found their place in that unwritten code to which a prompter obedience is rendered than to the most absolute of royal or imperial decrees.

But we are not limited to the comparatively rare and exceptional examples of primitive dexterity which the works of the palæolithic carver and etcher supply for illustrations of the special habit now under consideration. The graceful proportions and delicate manipulation of many of the chipped implements of flint have, not unnaturally, excited both admiration and wonder, in view of the very limited resources of the worker in flint.

But the process of the ancient arrow-maker is no lost art. It has been found in use among many barbarous races; and is still practised by some of the American Indian tribes, to whom the art has doubtless been transmitted through successive generations from remotest times. The modes of manufacture vary somewhat among different tribes; but they have been repeatedly witnessed and de-

scribed by explorers who have watched the native
arrow-maker at work ; and his operations no longer
present the difficulties which were long supposed
to beset this "lost art" of prehistoric times.
Among the rarer primitive implements are hammer-
stones, oblong or rounded in shape, generally with
cavities worked in two faces, so as to admit of their
being conveniently held between the finger and
thumb. Implements of this class have been repeatedly recovered from the French caves. An
interesting example occurred among the objects
embedded in the red cave-earth of Kents's Hole,
Devonshire ; and others of different periods, usually
quartzite pebbles or nodules of flint, have been
found in many localities. Some of them were
probably used in breaking the larger bones to
extract the marrow, but the battered edges of others
show their contact with harder material. Similar
hammer-stones occur in the Danish peat-mosses, in
the Swiss lake-dwellings, in sepulchral deposits, and
are also included among the implements of modern
savage art. They vary also in size, and were, no
doubt, applied to diverse purposes.

The mode of fashioning the large, tongue-shaped
implements and rude stone hatchets, which are

among the most characteristic drift implements, it can scarcely be doubted, was by blows of a stone or flint hammer; as was obviously the case with large unfinished flint or horn-stone implements recovered by me from some of the numerous pits of the Flint Ridge, a siliceous deposit of the Carboniferous Age which extends through the State of Ohio, from Newark to New Lexington. At various points along the ridge funnel-shaped pits occur, varying from four or five to fifteen feet deep; and similar traces of ancient mining may be seen in other localities, as at Leavenworth, about three hundred miles below Cincinnati, where the gray flint or chert abounds, of which large implements are chiefly made. The sloping sides of the pits are in many cases covered with the fractured flints, some of them partially shaped as if for manufacture. The work in the quarry was, no doubt, the mere rough fashioning of the flint by the tool-makers, with a view to facility of transport, in many cases, to distant localities. But the finer manipulation, by means of which the carefully-finished arrow-heads, knives, lances, hoes, drills, scrapers, etc., were manufactured, was reserved for leisurely and patient skill. Longfellow, in his

Indian epic, represents the Dacotah arrow-maker busy plying his craft. It was no doubt pursued by specially skilled workmen; for considerable dexterity is needed in striking the flakes from the flint core, and fashioning them into the nicely-finished edged tools and weapons to be seen in many museums. The choice of material is by no means limited to flint.

> At the doorway of his wigwam
> Sat the ancient Arrow-maker,
> In the land of the Dacotahs,
> Making arrow-heads of jasper,
> Arrow-heads of chalcedony.

Beautifully-finished arrow-heads and other smaller implements, fashioned of jasper, chalcedony, white quartz, and rock-crystal, are among the prized relics of many collections. The diversity of fracture in such materials must have taxed the skill of the expert workman, familiar chiefly with the regular cleavage of the obsidian, chert, or flint. But it is now known that the more delicate operations in the finishing of the flint implements were done by means of pressure with a horn or bone arrow-flaker; and not by a succession of blows with a chisel or hammer. The process has been repeatedly described by eye-witnesses. Dr. Evans quotes more than one account of methods pursued among the Eskimo, the native Mexicans, and the Shasta Indians of California. Another, and in some respects more minute account of the process, as it is in use by the Wintoon Indians, is furnished by Mr. B. B. Redding, in the *American Naturalist*, from his own personal observation. The material, as among the Shasta Indians, was obsidian; but the process is equally applicable to flint, the cleavage of which is nearly similar.

The artificer was Consolulu, the aged chief of the Wintoon Indians. His implements consisted of a deer-horn prong split lengthwise, four inches long and half an inch thick, with the semicircular end at right angles; two deer-horn prongs, one smaller than the other, with the ends ground down nearly to the shape of a square sharp-pointed file; and a piece of well-tanned buckskin, thick, soft, and pliable. Laying, as we are told, a lump of obsidian, about a pound in weight, in the palm of the left hand, he placed between the first and second fingers of the same hand the semi-cylindrical deer-horn implement, so that the straight side of one of the ends rested about a quarter of an inch from the edge of the block of obsidian. With a small water-worn

stone in his right hand, he struck the other end of
the prong, and a flake of obsidian was severed, well
adapted for the arrow-head.   On the buckskin, in
the palm of his left hand, he laid the obsidian flake,
which he held in place by the first three fingers of
that hand, and then took such a position on the
ground that the left elbow could rest on the left
knee and obtain a firm support.   Holding in his
right hand the larger of the two pointed prongs,
and resting his thumb on the side of his left hand
to serve as a fulcrum, he brought the point of the
prong about one-eighth of an inch within the edge
of the flake; and then, exerting a firm downward
pressure, fragment after fragment was broken off
until the edge of the arrow was made straight.   As
all the chips came off the lower edge, the cutting
edge was not yet in the centre of the side.   But
the Wintoon arrow-maker rubbed the side of the
prong repeatedly over the sharp edge, turned over
the flake, and, resuming the chipping as before,
brought the cutting edge to the centre.   In a
similar manner, the other side and the concave base
of the arrow-head were finished.   The formation
of indentations in the sides near the base for the
retention of the tendons to bind the arrow-head

securely to the shaft, apparently the most difficult
process, was in reality the easiest. The point of
the arrow-head was held between the thumb and
finger of the left hand, while the base rested on the
buckskin cushion in the palm. The point of the
smaller deer-horn prong, not exceeding one-sixteenth
of an inch square, was brought to bear on the part
of the side where the Indian arrow-maker considered
the notch should be. A sawing motion made the
chips fly to right and left, and in less than a minute
it was cut to the necessary depth. The other side
was then completed in like manner. The entire
process was accomplished, and the arrow-head
finished, in about forty minutes.

This account of the process of the Wintoon
arrow-maker refers, it will be seen, with a marked
though probably undesigned emphasis, to the use
of the right hand in all his active manipulations.
Its minute details are in other respects full of
interest from the light we may assume them to
throw on the method pursued by the primitive
implement makers of the earliest Stone Age. Dr.
Evans describes and figures a class of flint tools
recovered from time to time, the edges of which,
blunted and worn at both ends, suggest to his

experienced eye their probable use for chipping
out arrow-heads and other small implements of
flint, somewhat in the fashion detailed above, with
the tool of deer's horn.   To those accordingly he
applies the name of flaking tools, or fabricators.
But whether fashioned by means of flint or horn
fabricator, it is to be noted that the material to be
operated upon has to be held in one hand, while
the tool is dexterously manipulated with the other.
Signor Craveri, whose long residence in Mexico gave
him very favourable opportunities for observing the
process of the native workers in obsidian, remarks
that, when the Indians " wish to make an arrow or
other instrument of a splinter of obsidian, they take
the piece in the left hand, and hold grasped in the
other a small goat's horn.   They set this piece of
obsidian upon the horn, and dexterously pressing it
against the point of it, while they give the horn a
gentle movement from right to left, and up and
down, they disengage from it frequent chips; and
in this way obtain the desired form." [1]   Again, in
an account communicated to Sir Charles Lyell by
Mr. Cabot, of the mode of procedure of the Shasta
Indian arrow-makers, after describing the detach-

[1] Translated from Gastaldi.   See Evans's *Stone Implements*, p. 36.

ment of a piece from the obsidian pebble with the help of an agate chisel, he thus proceeds: " Holding the piece against the anvil with thumb and finger of his left hand, he commenced a series of blows, every one of which chipped off fragments of the brittle substance." The patient artificer worked upwards of an hour before he succeeded in producing a perfect arrow-head. His ingenious skill excited the admiration of the spectator, who adds the statement that among the Indians of California arrow-making is a distinct profession, in which few attain excellence.

The point noticeable here in reference to the accounts given by the various observers is the uniform assumption of right-handedness. Mr. Redding, Signor Craveri, and Mr. Cabot not only agree in describing the block of obsidian as held in the left hand, while the tools are employed in the right hand to fashion it into shape; but the whole language, especially in the description given by Signor Craveri, assumes right-handedness as not only the normal, but the invariable characteristic of the worker in stone. In reality, however, an ingenious investigator, Mr. F. H. Cushing of the Smithsonian Institution, while engaged in a series

of tentative experiments to determine the process of
working in flint and obsidian, had his attention
accidentally called to the fact that the primitive
implements of the Stone Age perpetuate for us a
record of the use of one or the other hand in their
manufacture. With the instinctive zeal of youthful
enthusiasm Mr. Cushing, while still a boy on his
father's farm in Western New York, carried out a
systematic series of flint workings with a view to
ascertain for himself the process by which the
ancient arrow-makers fashioned the flint implements
that then excited his interest. After repeated
failures in his attempts to chip the flint into the
desired shape by striking off fragments with a stone
hammer, he accidentally discovered that small flakes
could be detached from the flint core with great
certainty and precision by pressure with a pointed
rod of bone or horn; and, as I have recently learned
from him, the instrument employed by him in those
experiments was the same as that which Dr. John
Evans informs me he accidentally hit upon in his
earliest successful efforts at flint-arrow making, viz.
a tooth-brush handle. In thus employing a bone
or horn flaker, the sharp edge of the flake cuts
slightly into the bone; and when the latter is

E

twisted suddenly upward, a small scale flies off at
the point of pressure in a direction which can be
foreseen and controlled.   With this discovery the
essential process of arrow-making had been mastered.
Spear and arrow-heads could be flaked with the
most delicate precision, with no such liability to
fracture as leads to constant failure in any attempt
to chip even the larger and ruder spear or axe-heads
into shape.   The hammer-stone only suffices for the
earlier processes, including the detachment of the
flake from the rough flint nodule, and trimming it
roughly into the required form, preparatory to the
delicate manipulation of edging, pointing, and notch-
ing the arrow-head.   The thinning of the flint-blade
is effected by detaching long thin scales or flakes
from the surface by using the flaker like a chisel
and striking it a succession of blows with a hammer-
stone.   The marks of this delicate surface-flaking
are abundantly manifest on the highly-finished
Danish knives, daggers, and large spear-heads, as
well as upon most other flint implements of Europe's
Neolithic Age.   The large spear and tongue-shaped
implements of the drift are, on the contrary, rudely
chipped, evidently by the blows of a hammer-stone ;
although some of the more delicately fashioned drift

implements seem to indicate that the use of the
flint or bone flaker was not unknown to the men
of the Palæolithic Age.   But the chipping-stone or
hammer was in constant use at the later period;
and the small hammer-stone, with indentations on
its sides for the finger and thumb, and its rounded
edges marked with the evidence of long use in
chipping the flint nodules into the desired forms,
abounds both in Europe and America, wherever the
arrow-maker has carried on his primitive art.   The
implements in use varied with the available material.
A T-shaped wooden flaker sufficed for the Aztecs in
shaping the easily-worked obsidian.   The jasper,
chalcedony, and quartz, in like manner, yield readily
to the pressure of a slender flaker of horn; whereas
Mr. Cushing notes that the "tough horn-stone of
Western Arctic America could not be flaked by
pressure in the hand, but must be rested against
some solid substance, and flaked by means of an
instrument, the handle of which fitted the palm like
that of an umbrella, enabling the operator to exert
a pressure against the substance to be chipped
nearly equal to the weight of the body."   One
result of Mr. Cushing's experiments in arrow-making
was to satisfy him that the greatest difficulty was to

make long narrow surface-flakes. Hence, contrary to all preconceived ideas, it is easier to form the much-prized, delicately-finished small arrow-head, with barbs and stem, than larger and seemingly ruder implements which involve much surface-flaking.

It is interesting to learn of the recovery of this lost art of the ancient arrow-makers by a series of tentative experiments independently pursued by different observers. Before Mr. Cushing's attention had been directed to any of the descriptions of the process of modern flint-workers, now familiar to us, he aimed at placing himself in the same condition as the primitive manufacturer of Europe's Stone Age, or of the ancient Mound Builders of North America, devoid of metallic tools, and with the flint, obsidian, jasper, or hornstone, as the most available material out of which to fashion nearly all needful implements. He set to work accordingly with no other appliances than such sticks and variously shaped stones as could be found on the banks of the streams where he sought his materials. The results realise to us, in a highly interesting way, the earliest stages in the training of the self-taught workman of the Palæolithic Age. After

making various implements akin to the most rudely
fashioned examples from the river-drift or the old
flint pits, by means of chipping one flint or stone
with another, he satisfied himself that no amount of
chipping, however carefully practised, would produce
surfaces like the best of those which he was trying
to imitate.   He accordingly assumed that there
must be some other process unknown to him.   By
chance he tried pressure with the point of a stick,
instead of chipping with a stone, and the mystery
was solved.   He had hit on nearly the same method
already described as in use by Aztecs, Eskimos, and
Red Indians ; and found that he could fashion the
fractured flint or obsidian into nearly any shape
that he desired.   As has been already noted, Mr.
Cushing, like Dr. Evans, resorted subsequently to
the easily available tool furnished by the handle
of a tooth-brush.   Having thus mastered the secret
of the old flint-workers, he succeeded before long
in the manufacture of well-finished arrows, spear-
heads, and daggers of flint, closely resembling the
products of the primitive workmen both of the Old
and the New World.

Thus far the results accord with other investigations : but in the course of his operations Mr.

Cushing also noted this fact, that the grooves produced by the flaking of the flint or obsidian all
turned in one direction. This proved to be due to
the constant use of his right hand. When the
direction of pressure by the bone or stick was
reversed, the result was apparent in the opposite
direction of the grooves. So far as his observations
then extended, he occasionally found an arrow-head
or other primitive stone implement with the flake
grooves running from left to right, showing, as he
believed, the manipulation of a left-handed workman ;
but, from the rarity of their occurrence, it might be
concluded that, as a rule, prehistoric man was right-
handed. When Mr. Cushing reported the results
of those investigations into the arts of the Stone
Age, at a meeting of the Anthropological Society of
Washington in May 1879, Professor Mason confirmed from his own observation the occurrence of
flint implements indicating by the reversed direction
of the bevelling that they were produced by left-
handed workmen. Mr. Cushing further notes that
" arrow-making is accompanied by great fatigue and
profuse perspiration. It has a prostrating effect
upon the nervous system, which shows itself again
in the direction of fracture. The first fruits of the

workman's labour, while still fresh and vigorous,
can be distinguished from the implements produced
after he had become exhausted at his task; and it
is thus noteworthy that on an unimpressible substance like flint even the moods and passions of
long-forgotten centuries may be found thus traced
and recorded."

In an ingenious brochure by Mr. Charles Reade,
styled "The Coming Man," specially aiming at the
development in the rising generation of the use of
the left hand, so that the man of the future shall
be ambidextrous or "either-handed," he remarks:
"There certainly is amongst mankind a vast weight
of opinion against my position that man is by
nature as either-handed as an ape; and that custom
should follow nature. The majority believe the left
arm and hand inferior to the right in three things:
power, dexterity, and dignity. Nor is this notion
either old-fashioned or new-fangled. It is many
thousand years old; and comes down by unbroken
descent to the present day." The writer then goes
on to affirm: "It has never existed amongst rank
barbarians; it is not indicated in the genuine flint
instruments; but only in those which modern
dexterity plants in old strata, to delight and defraud

antiquarians; and the few primitive barbarians that
now remain, living relics of the Stone Age, use both
arms indifferently." The conclusions here assumed
as established by evidence derived from the study of
"the genuine flint instruments" imply, I presume,
that they do embody indications of right and left-
hand manipulation in nearly equal proportions;
whereas the forgeries of the modern "Flint Jack"
all betray evidence of right-handed manufacture,
and of consequent modernness. This, however,
must have been set forth as a mere surmise; for, as
now appears, it is in conflict with the results of
careful investigations directed to the products of the
primitive flint workers. The opinion adopted by
Mr. Cushing, after repeated observation and tentative experiment, is that primitive man was, as a
rule, right-handed. The evidence adduced is insufficient for an absolute determination of the
question; but any strongly-marked examples of the
left-handed workman's art thus far observed among
palæolithic flint implements appear to be exceptional.
No higher authority than Dr. John Evans can be
appealed to in reference to the manipulations of the
primitive flint-worker, and, in writing to me on the
subject, he remarks: "I think that there is some

evidence of the flint-workers of old having been
right-handed; the particular twist, both in some
palæolithic implements, as in one in my own pos-
session from Hoxne, and in some American rifled
arrow-heads, being due to the manner of chipping,
and being most in accordance with their being held
in the left hand and chipped with the right." In
the detailed description, given in his *Ancient Stone
Implements of Great Britain*, of the example from
Hoxne above referred to, Dr. John Evans remarks :
" It presents the peculiarity, which is by no means
uncommon in ovate implements, of having the side
edges not in one plane, but forming a sort of ogee
curve. In this instance the blade is twisted to
such an extent that a line drawn through the two
edges near the point is at an angle of at least 45°
to a line through the edges at the broadest part of
the implement. I think," he adds, " that this twisting of the edges was not in this case intended to
serve any particular purpose, but was rather the
accidental result of the method pursued in chipping
the flint into its present form."[1] A similar curvature is seen in a long-pointed implement from
Reculver, in the collection of Mr. J. Brent, F.S.A.,

[1] *Ancient Stone Implements*, p. 520.

and again in another large example of this class,
from Hoxne in Suffolk, presented to the Society of
Antiquaries of London upwards of eighty years ago.
This, as Dr. Evans notes, exhibits the same peculiarity
of the twisting of the edges so markedly, and indeed
so closely resembles the specimen in his own collection, that they might have been made by the same
hand.   Of another example, from Santon Downham,
near Hetford, Suffolk, almond-shaped, and with
dendritic markings in evidence of its palæolithic
date, Dr. Evans remarks : " It is fairly symmetrical
in contour with an edge all round, which is somewhat blunted at the base.   This edge, however, is
not in one plane, but considerably curved, so that
when seen sideways it forms an ogee curve ;" and
he adds : " I have other implements of the same,
and of more pointed forms, with similarly curved
edges, both from France and other parts of England,
but whether this curvature was intentional it is
impossible to say.   In some cases it is so marked
that it can hardly be the result of accident ; and
the curve is, so far as I have observed, almost
without exception ઠ, and not S.   If not intentional,
the form may be the result of all the blows by
which the implement was finally chipped out having

been given on the one face on one side, and on
the opposite on the other."[1]   In other words, the
implement-maker worked throughout with the flaker
in the same hand; and that hand, with very rare
exceptions, appears to have been the right hand.
The evidence thus far adduced manifestly points to
the predominance of right-handed men among the
palæolithic flint-workers.   For if the flint-arrow
maker, working apart, and with no motive, therefore,
suggested by the necessity of accommodating himself
to a neighbouring workman, has habitually used the
right hand from remote palæolithic times, it only
remains to determine the origin of a practice too
nearly invariable to have been the result of accident.
This, however, has long eluded research; or thus
far, at least, has been ascribed to very different
causes.   But to any who regards the special inquiry
now under review as one worthy of further consideration, the class of implements referred to offers
a trustworthy source of evidence whereby to arrive
at a relative estimate of the prevalent use of one or
the other hand among uncultured races of men, alike
in ancient and modern times.

Dr. Evans has figured and described what he

[1] *Ancient Stone Implements*, p. 501.

believes to have been the flaking tools or fabricators
in earliest use among the flint-workers for chipping
out arrow-heads and other small implements.   They
are fashioned of the same material ; and some of
them are carefully wrought into a form best adapted
for being held in the hand of the workman.   Specimens of the bone arrow-flakers in use by the Eskimo
workers in flint are also familiar to us.   Different
forms of those instruments are engraved among the
illustrations to *The Ancient Stone Implements, Weapons,
and Ornaments of Great Britain,* from specimens in
the Blackmore Museum and the Christy Collection ;[1]
and Dr. Evans describes the mode of using them as
witnessed by Sir Edward Belcher among the Eskimo
of Cape Lisburne, but without reference to the point
now alluded to.   Dr. John Rae, who, like myself, is
inveterately left-handed, informs me that, without
having taken particular notice of Indian or Eskimo
practice in the use of one or the other hand, he
observed that some among them were markedly
ambidextrous.   But, he adds, " from a curious
story told me by an Eskimo about a bear throwing
a large piece of ice at the head of a walrus, and
telling me as a noteworthy fact that he threw it

[1] *Ancient Stone Implements,* figs. 8, 9, 10.

with the left forepaw, as if it were something un-usual, it would seem to indicate that left-handedness was not very common among the Eskimos." It shows, at any rate, that the Eskimo noted the use of the left paw as something diverse from the normal practice. But if the deductions based on the experimental working in flint are well founded, the test supplied by the direction of the flaking grooves of obsidian, chert, or flint implements will be equally available for determining the prevalent use of one or other hand by the Eskimo and other modern savage races, as among those of the Palæo-lithic and Neolithic Periods.

CHAPTER V

THE DISHONOURED HAND

AN interesting discovery made in recent years in the course of some researches into the traces of the neolithic flint-workers of Norfolk invites attention from the evidence it has been thought to furnish of the traces of a left-handed workman of that remote era.

The Rev. William Greenwell carried out a series of explorations of a number of flint-pits, known as Grimes's Graves, near Brandon, in Norfolk; and in a communication to the Ethnological Society of London on the subject, he states that in clearing out one of the primitive subterranean galleries excavated in the chalk by the British workmen of the Neolithic Age, in order to procure flint nodules in a condition best adapted for their purpose, it was

found that, while the pits were still being worked,
the roof of the gallery had given way and blocked
up its whole width. The removal of this obstruction disclosed three recesses extending beyond the
face of the chalk, at the end of the gallery, which
had been excavated by the ancient miners in pro-
curing the flint. In front of two of these recesses
thus hollowed out lay two picks corresponding to
others found in various parts of the shafts and
galleries, made from the antlers of the red deer.
But Canon Greenwell noted that, while the handle
of each was laid towards the mouth of the gallery,
the tines which formed the blades of the picks
pointed towards each other, showing, as he con-
ceived, that in all probability they had been used
respectively by a right and a left-handed man.
The day's work over, the men had laid down their
tools, ready for the next day's work; meanwhile
the roof had fallen in, and the picks were left there
undisturbed through all the intervening centuries,
till the reopening of the gallery in our own day.

The chronicles of the neolithic miners of Norfolk, as of the greatly more ancient flint-workers of
the drift, or the draftsmen of the Dordogne, are
recorded for us in very definite characters, more

trustworthy, but unfortunately as meagre as other early chronicles. But when we come within the range of written records, or analyse the evidence that language supplies among unlettered races, a flood of light is thrown on the subject of a discriminating choice in use of one or the other hand. The evidence derived from this source leaves no room for doubt that the preferential choice is no mere habit; but that everywhere, among barbarous and civilised races alike, one specific hand has been assigned for all actions requiring either unusual force or special delicacy.

Even among races in the rudest condition of savage life, such as the Australians and the Pacific Islanders, terms for " right," the " right hand," or approximate expressions show that the distinction is no product of civilisation. In the Kamilarai dialect of the Australians bordering on Hunter's River and Lake Maquaria *matara* signifies " hand," but they have the terms *turovn*, right, on the right hand, and *ngorangón*, on the left hand. In the Wiraturai dialect of the Wellington Valley the same ideas are expressed by the words *bumalgál* and *miraga*, dextrorsum and sinistrorsum.

The idea lying at the root of our own decimal

notation, which has long since been noted by
Lepsius, Donaldson, and other philologists, as the
source of names of Greek and Latin numerals, is
no less discernible in the rudest savage tongues.
Among the South Australians the simple names for
numerals are limited to two, viz. *ryup*, one, and
politi, two; the two together express "three";
politi-politi, four; and then "five" is indicated by
the term *ryup-murnangin*, *i.e.* one hand; ten by
politi-murnangin, *i.e.* two hands. The same idea is
apparent in the dialects of Hawaii, Raratonga, Viti,
and New Zealand, in the use of the one term:
lima, rima, linga, ringa, etc., for hand and for the
number five. *Fulu* and its equivalents stand for
"ten," apparently from the root *fu*, whole, altogether;
while the word *tau*, which in the Hawaiian signifies
"ready," in the Tahitian "right, proper," and in the
New Zealand, "expert, dexterous," is the common
Polynesian term for the right hand. In the Vitian
language, as spoken in various dialects throughout
the Viti or Fiji Islands, the distinction is still more
explicitly indicated. There is first the common
term *linga*, the hand, or arm; then the ceremonial
term *daka*, employed exclusively in speaking of that
of a chief, but which, it may be presumed, also

F

expresses the right hand ; as, while there is no other
word for it, a distinct term *sema* is the left hand.
The root *se* is found not only in the Viti, but also
in the Samoa, Tonga, Mangariva, and New Zealand
dialects, signifying "to err, to mistake, to wander";
semo, unstable, unfixed; while there is the word
matau, right, dexter, clearly proving the recognition
of the distinction. In the case of the Viti or
Fijian, this is the more noticeable, as there appears
to be some reason for believing that left-handedness
is exceptionally prevalent among the natives of the
Fiji Islands. In 1876 a correspondent of the
Times communicated a series of letters to that
journal, in which he embodied anthropological notes
on the Fijians, obtained both from his own observations during repeated visits to the Islands, and from
conversation with English, American, and German
settlers, at the port of call, and on the route between
San Francisco and the Australian colonies. "The
Fijians," he says, "are quite equal in stature to
white men; they are better developed relatively in
the chest and arms than in the lower limbs; they
are excellent swimmers, and, if trained, are good
rowers. Left-handed men are more common among
them than among white people; three were pointed

out in one little village near the anchorage." Yet here, as elsewhere, it is exceptional. Vague statements from time to time appear, affirming a prevalence of left-handedness among certain barbarous races. A writer in the *Medical Record* in 1886 says : " No purely left-handed race has ever been discovered, although there seems to be a difference in different tribes. Seventy per cent of the inhabitants of the Punjab use the left hand by preference ; and the greater number of the Hottentots and Bushmen of South Africa also use the left hand in preference to the right." But such statements, to be of any value, must be based on carefully accumulated evidence, such as is scarcely accessible in relation to nomad savage tribes. Such comprehensive generalisations generally prove to have no better foundation than the exceptional and chance observations of a traveller. It is otherwise when the evidence is derived from language, or from the observation of traders or missionaries long resident among the people.

Throughout the widely scattered islands of the Pacific the recognition of native right-handedness as the normal usage is confirmed alike by trustworthy witnesses and by the definite evidence of language.

The Samoan word *lima*, hand, also signifying "five," and the terms *lima maira*, right hand, and *lima woat*, left hand, are used as the equivalents of our own mode of expression. But also the left hand is *lima tau-anga-vale*, literally, the hand that takes hold foolishly. In the case of the Samoans, it may be added, as well as among the natives of · New Britain and other of the Pacific islands, the favoured hand corresponds with our right hand. My informant, the Rev. George Brown, for fourteen years a missionary in Polynesia, states that the distinction of right and left hand is as marked as among Europeans; and left-handedness is altogether exceptional. In the Terawan language, which is spoken throughout the group of islands on the equator called the Kingsmill Archipelago, the terms *atai* or *edai*, right, dexter, (entirely distinct from *rapa*, good, right,) and *maan*, left, sinister, are applied to *bai*, or *pai*, the hand, to denote the difference, *e.g. te bai maan*, the left hand, literally, the "dirty hand," that which is not used in eating. The languages of the American continent furnish similar evidence of the recognition of the distinction among its hunter-tribes. In the Chippeway the word for "my right hand" is *ne-keche-neenj*, *ne* being the prenominal prefix, literally, " my great hand." " My left hand " is *ne-nuh-munje-neenj-ne. Numunj* is the same root as appears in *nuh-munj-e-doon*, " I do not know ; " and the idea obviously is " the uncertain or unreliable hand." Again, in the Mohawk language, " the right hand " is expressed by the term *ji-ke-we-yen-den-dah-kon*, from *ke-we-yen-deh*, literally, " I know how." *Ji* is a particle conveying the idea of *side*, and the termination *dah-kon* has the meaning of " being accustomed to." It is, therefore, the limb accustomed to act promptly, the dexterous organ. *Ske-ne-kwa-dih*, the left hand, literally means " the other side."

Analogous terms are found alike in the languages of civilised and barbarous races, expressing the same inferiority of one hand in relation to the other which is indicated in the classical *sinistra* as the subordinate of the *dextra manus*. The honourable significance of the right hand receives special prominence in the most sacred allusions of the Hebrew scriptures ; and in mediæval art the right hand in benediction is a frequent symbol of the First Person of the Trinity. In the Anglo-Saxon version of the New Testament the equivalent terms appear as

swythre and *wynstre*, as in Matthew vi. 3 : " Sothlice
thonne thu thinne aelmessan do, nyte thin wynstre
hwaet do thin swythre ; " " When thou doest alms, let
not thy left hand know what thy right hand doeth."
Again the distinction appears in a subsequent
passage thus : " And he geset tha scep on hys
swithran healfe, and tha tyccenu on hys wynstran
healfe " (Matthew xxv. 34). Here the derivation of
swythre from *swyth*, strong, powerful, *swythra*, a
strong one, a dexterous man, *swythre*, the stronger,
the right hand, is obvious enough. It is also used
as an adjective, as in Matthew v. 30 : " And gif
thin *swythre hand* the aswice, aceorf hig of ; " " And
if thy right hand offend thee, cut it off." The
derivation of *wynstre* is less apparent, and can only
be referred to its direct significance, *se wynstra*, the
left. In the Greek we find the isolated ἀριστερός,
ἀριστερά, left, ἡ ἀριστερά, the left hand. Whatever etymology we adopt for this word, the depreciatory comparison between the left and the more
favoured δεξιά, or right hand, is obvious enough in
the σκαιός, the left, the ill-omened, the unlucky ;
σκαιότης, left-handedness, awkwardness ; like the
French *gauche*, awkward, clumsy, uncouth. The
Greek had also the term derived from the left arm

as the shield-bearer; hence ἐπ' ἀσπίδα, on the left
or shield side.

The Gaelic has supplied to Lowland Scotland the
term *ker*, or carry-handed, in common use, derived
from *lamh-chearr*, the left hand.   In the secondary
meanings attached to *ker*, or carry, it signifies awkward, devious; and in a moral sense is equivalent
to the English use of the word "sinister."   To
"*gang the kar gate*" is to go the left road, *i.e.* the
wrong road, or the road to ruin.   There is no
separate word in the Gaelic for "right hand," but it
is called *lamh dheas* and *lamh ceart*.   Both words
imply "proper, becoming, or right."   *Ceart* is the
common term to express what is right, correct, or
fitting, whereas *dheas* primarily signifies the "south,"
and is explained by the supposed practice of the
Druid augur following the sun in his divinations.
In this it will be seen to agree with the secondary
meaning of the Hebrew *yamin*, and to present a
common analogy with the corresponding Greek and
Latin terms hereafter referred to.   *Deisal*, a com-
pound of *dheas*, south, and *iul*, a guide, a course, is
commonly used as an adjective, to express a lucky
or favourable occurrence.   The "left hand" is
variously styled *lamh chli*, the wily or cunning

hand, and *lamh cearr*, or *ciotach*.   *Cearr* is wrong,
unlucky, and *ciotach* is the equivalent of *sinister*,
formed from the specific name for the left hand,
ciotag, Welsh *chwithig*.   According to Pliny,[1] "the
Gauls, in their religious rites, contrary to the practice
of the Romans, turned to the left."   An ancient
Scottish tradition traces the surname of Kerr to the
fact that the Dalriadic king, Kynach-Ker or Conn-
chad Cearr, as he is called in the *Duan Albanach*,
was left-handed; though the name is strongly suggestive of a term of reproach like that of the Saxon
Ethelred, the Unready.

Milton in one of his Sonnets plays in sportive
satire with the name of another left-handed Scot,
" Colkitto, or Macdonnel, or Galasp."   The person
referred to under the first name was the Earl of
Antrim's deputy, by whom the invasion of Scotland
was attempted in 1644 on behalf of the Stuarts.
The name is scarcely less strange in its genuine
form of Alastair MacCholla-Chiotach; that is, Alex-
ander, son of Coll, the left-handed.   This was the
elder Macdonnel, of Colonsay, who was noted for
his ability to wield his claymore with equal dexterity
in the left hand or the right; or, as one tradition

[1] *Hist. Nat.* lib. xxviii. c. 2.

affirms, for his skill as a left-handed swordsman after the loss of his right hand; and hence his sobriquet of Colkittock, or Coll, the Left-handed. The term " carry " is frequently used in Scotland as one implying reproach or contempt. In some parts of the country, and especially in Lanarkshire, it is even regarded as an evil omen to meet a carry-handed person when setting out on a journey. Jamieson notes the interjectional phrase *car-shamye* (Gaelic *sgeamh-aim*, to reproach) as in use in Kinross-shire in the favourite Scottish game of shinty, when an antagonist takes what is regarded as an undue advantage by using his club in the left hand.

All this, while indicating the exceptional character of left-handedness, clearly points to a habit of such frequent occurrence as to be familiarly present to every mind. But the exceptional skill, or dexterity, as it may be fitly called, which usually pertains to the left-handed operator is generally sufficient to redeem him from slight. The ancient Scottish game of golf, which is only a more refined and strictly regulated form of the rustic shinty, is one in which the implements are of necessity right-handed, and so subject the left-handed player to great disadvantage, unless he provides his own special clubs. The links at Leith have long been famous as an arena for Scottish golfers. King Charles I. was engaged in a game of golf there when, in November 1641, a letter was delivered into his hands which gave him the first account of the Irish Rebellion. The same links were a favourite resort of his younger son, James II., while still Duke of York; and some curious traditions preserve the memory of his relish for the game. There, accordingly, golf is still played with keenest zest; and among its present practisers is a left-handed golfer, who, as usual with left-handed persons, is practically ambidextrous. He has accordingly provided himself with a double set of right and left drivers and irons; so that he can use either hand at pleasure according to the character of the ground, or the position of the ball, to the general discomfiture of his one-handed rivals. The Scotchmen of Montreal and Quebec have transplanted the old national game to Canadian soil; and the latter city has a beautiful course on the historical battle-field, the scene of Wolfe's victory and death. Their experience induced the Quebec Golf Club, when ordering spare sets of implements for the use of occasional guests from Great Britain,

to consider the propriety of providing a left-handed
set.   In the discussion to which the proposal gave
rise, it was urged to be unnecessary, as a left-handed
player generally has his own clubs with him; but
finally the order was limited to two left-handed
drivers, so that when a left-handed golfer joins them
he has to put with his driver.   This considerateness
of the Quebec golfers was no doubt stimulated by
the fact that there is a skilled golfer of the Montreal
Club whose feats of dexterity as a left-handed
player at times startle them.   A Quebec golfer
writes to me thus: "There is one left-handed
fellow belonging to the Montreal Club who comes
down occasionally to challenge us; and I have
watched his queer play with a good deal of interest
and astonishment."

To the left-handed man his right hand is the
less ready, the less dexterous, and the weaker member.   But in all ordinary experience the idea of
weakness, uncertainty, unreliability, attaches to the
left hand, and so naturally leads to the tropical
significance of "unreliable, untrustworthy," in a
moral sense.   Both ideas are found alike in barbarous and classic languages.   An interesting example
of the former occurs in Ovid's *Fasti* (iii. 869),

where the poet speaks of the flight of Helle and her
brother on the golden-fleeced ram; and describes her
as grasping its horn "with her feeble left hand,
when she made of herself a name for the waters,"
i.e. by falling off and being drowned—

> Utque fugam capiant, aries nitidissimus auro
> Traditur. Ille vehit per freta longa duos.
> Dicitur informa cornu tenuisse sinistra
> Femina, cum de se nomina fecit aquæ.

In the depreciatory moral sense, Plautus in the
Persa (II. ii. 44) calls the left hand *furtifica*,
"thievish." "Estne hæc manus? Ubi illa altera
est furtifica læva?" So in like manner the term in
all its forms acquires a depreciatory significance, and
is even applied to sinister looks. So far, then, as
the evidence of language goes, the distinction of the
right from the left hand, as the more reliable member, appears to be coeval with the earliest known
use of language.

CHAPTER VI

THE PRIMITIVE ABACUS

UNDER varying aspects of the question of right-handedness the inquiries into its origin have naturally reverted to the lateral position of the heart as a probable source of diversity of action in the two hands; and this is the more suggestive owing to the fact that exceptional cases of its reversed position are occasionally found. When Carlyle reflected on right-handedness as "probably the oldest human institution that exists," he suggested as the source of choice of the hand that it "probably arose in fighting: most important," as he says, "to protect your heart and its adjacencies, and to carry the shield on the hand." This idea, in so far as it implies the habitual use of the shield in the left hand, or on the left arm, and consequently of the shield-hand as

left and passive, is old as Homer; and the evidence
of its practice is abundantly confirmed by the
drawings on the most archaic Greek vases.   The
right side was ἐπὶ δόρυ, the spear side, while the
left was ἐπ' ἀσπίδα, the shield side.   The familiar
application of the terms in this sense is seen in
Xenophon's *Anabasis*, IV. iii. 26 : Καὶ παρήγγειλε
τοῖς λοχαγοῖς κατ' ἐνωμοτίας ποιήσασθαι ἕκαστον
τὸν ἑαυτοῦ λόχον, παρ' ἀσπίδας παραγαγόντας τὴν
ἐνωμοτίαν ἐπὶ φάλαγγος, " He ordered to draw up
his century in squads of twenty-five, and post them
in line to the left."   And again, *Anabasis*, IV. iii.
29 : Τοῖς δὲ παρ' ἑαυτῷ παρήγγειλεν . . . ἀναστρέ-
ψαντας ἐπὶ δόρυ, κ.τ.λ., " He ordered his own
division, turning to the right," etc.   Egyptian
paintings are older than the earliest Greek vases,
but they are less reliable; for in the symmetrical
arrangements of hieroglyphic paintings the groups
of figures are habitually reversed, right and left,
looking toward a central line or point.   Yet there
also evidence may be found confirming the same
idea.

But we may once more turn aside from the
physical to the intellectual aspect of available
evidence, and find confirmation of a like kind in one

of the earliest definite manifestations of cultured reason.   Few tests of relative stages of civilisation are more trustworthy than that of the definite conception of high numbers.   The prevalence of a decimal system of numerals among widely severed nations, alike in ancient and modern times, has been universally ascribed to the simple process of counting with the aid of the fingers.   Mr. Francis Galton, in his *Narrative of an Exploration in Tropical Africa*, when describing the efforts of the Damaras at computation, states that the mental effort fails them beyond *three*.   " When they wish to express *four*, they take to their fingers, which are to them as formidable instruments of calculation as a sliding rule is to an English schoolboy.   They puzzle very much after *five*, because no spare hand remains to grasp and secure the fingers that are required for units." Turning to the line of evidence which this primitive method of computation suggests, some striking analogies reveal a recognition of ideas common to the savage and to the cultivated Greek and Roman. Donaldson, in his *New Cratylus*, in seeking to trace the first ten numerals to their primitive roots in Sanskrit, Zend, Greek, and Latin, derives seven of them from the three primitive prenominal elements.

But *five*, *nine*, and *ten* are referred by him directly
to the same infantile source of decimal notation,
suggested by the ten fingers, as has been recognised
in similar operation among the Hawaiians, and the
Maoris of New Zealand. " One would fancy, indeed,
without any particular investigation of the subject,
that the number *five* would have some connection
with the word signifying ' a hand,' and the number
ten with a word denoting the 'right hand '; for in
counting with our fingers we begin with the little
finger of the left hand."   Hence the familiar idea,
as expressed in its simplest form, where Hesiod (*Op.*
740) calls the hand πέντοζον, the five-branch ; and
hence also πεμπάζω, primarily to count on five
fingers.

Bopp, adopting the same idea, considers the
Sanskrit *pan'-cha* as formed of the copulative conjunction added to the neuter form of *pa*, one, and so
signifying " and one."   Benary explains it as an
abbreviation of *pán'-i-cha*, " and the hand "—the
conjunction being equally recognisable in *pan'-cha*,
πέν-τε, and *quinque*.   This, they assume, expressed
the idea that the enumerator then began to count
with the other hand ; but Donaldson ingeniously
suggests the simpler meaning, that after counting

four the whole hand was opened and held up. To
reckon by the hand was, accordingly, to make a
rough computation, as in the *Wasps* of Aristo-
phanes, where Bdelycleon bids his father, the dicast,
" first of all calculate roughly, not by pebbles, but
ἀπὸ χειρός, with the hand."

The relation of δεξιά to δέκ-α and *dextra*, δέκ-α,
decem, δεκ-σιός, *decster*, illustrates the same idea.
Grimm, indeed, says, " In counting with the fingers,
one naturally begins with the left hand, and so goes
on to the right. This may explain why, in different
languages, the words for *the left* refer to the root of
five, those for *the right* to the root of *ten*." Hence
also the derivation of finger, through the Gothic
and Old High German, from the stem for " five "
and " left "; while the Greek and Latin, δάκτυλος
and *digitus*, are directly traceable to δέκα and *decem*.
The connection between ἀριστερά and *sinistra* is
also traced with little difficulty : the sibilant of the
latter being ascribed to an initial digamma, assumed
in the archaic form of the parent vocabulary. Nor
is the relationship of δεξιά with *digitus* a far-fetched
one. As the antique custom was to hand the wine
from right to left, so it may be presumed that the
ancients commenced counting with the left hand, in

the use of that primitive abacus, finishing with the
dexter or right hand at the tenth digit, and so
completing the decimal numeration.

The inferior relation of the left to the right
hand was also indicated in the use of the former
for lower, and the latter for higher numbers beyond
ten. In reckoning with their fingers, both Greeks
and Romans counted on the left hand as far as a
hundred, then on the right hand to two hundred,
and so on alternately: the even numbers being
always reckoned on the right hand. The poet
Juvenal refers to this in his tenth Satire, where,
in dwelling on the attributes of age, he speaks of
the centenarian, "who counts his years on his right
hand "—

> Felix nimirum, qui tot per secula mortem
> Distulit, atque suos jam dextra computat annos,
> Quique novum toties mustum bibit.

A curious allusion, by Tacitus, in the first book
of his *History*, serves to show that the German
barbarians beyond the Alps no less clearly recognised the significance of the right hand as that
which was preferred, and accepted as the more
honourable member. The Lingones, a Belgian
tribe, had sent presents to the legions, as he

narrates : and in accordance with ancient usage
gave as the symbolical emblem of friendship two
right hands clasped together. "Miserat civitas
Lingonum vetere instituto dona legionibus, dextras,
hospitii insigne." The dextræ are represented on
a silver quinarius of Julius Cæsar, thus described
in Ackerman's *Catalogue of rare and unedited
Roman Coins*, "PAX. S. C. Female head. *Rev.* L.
AEMILIVS. BVCA. IIII. VIR. Two hands
joined." [1]

Other evidence of a different kind confirms the
recognition and preferential use of the right hand
among our Teutonic ancestors from the remotest
period. Dr. Richard Lepsius, in following out an
ingenious analysis of the primitive names for the
numerals, and the sources of their origin, traces
from the common Sanskrit root *daça*, Greek δέκα,
through the Gothic *taihun*, the *hunda*, as in *tva
hunda*, two hundred. He next points out the re-
semblance between the Gothic *hunda* and *handus*,
i.e. "the hand," showing that this is no accidental
agreement, but that the words are etymologically
one and the same. The A.S. *hund*, a hundred,
originally meant only "ten," and was prefixed to

[1] Ackerman, i. 106.

numerals above twenty, as *hund-eahtatig*, eighty, *hund-teontig*, a hundred, etc.

Thus far philological evidence clearly points to a very wide prevalence of the recognition of right-handedness; and when we turn from this to the oldest sources of direct historical evidence, the references abundantly confirm the same conclusions. The earliest ascertained historical record of left-handed dexterity is familiar to all. The references to this in the Book of Judges show that the skill of the left-handed among the tribe of Benjamin was specially noted, while at the same time the very form of the record marks the attribute as exceptional; and all the more so as occurring in the tribe whose patronymic—*ben yamin*, the son of the right hand,—so specially indicates the idea of honour and dignity constantly associated with the right hand throughout the Hebrew Scriptures. When, as we read in the Book of Judges, the Lord raised up as a deliverer of Israel from the oppression of Eglon, King of Moab, Ehud, the son of Gera, he was a Benjamite, a man left-handed. He accordingly fashioned for himself a two-edged dagger, which he girt under his raiment upon his right thigh; and thus armed he presented him-

self as the bearer of a present from the children
of Israel to the king, and sought a private inter-
view, saying, "I have a secret errand unto thee,
O king." The special fitness of the left-handed
emissary, as best suited for the daring act required
of him, is in itself a proof that it was an exceptional
attribute. The express mention that he girded his
dagger on his right thigh is significant. It was
doubtless assumed that when he reached with his
left hand towards the weapon concealed under his
raiment, the motion would not excite suspicion.
A later chapter of the same venerable historical
record furnishes the account of a body of seven
hundred chosen marksmen, all left-handed, selected
from the same tribe for their pre-eminent skill.
The incident is noteworthy, and recalls the mode
of selection of the three hundred chosen men with
whom Gideon overthrew the Midianites. As the
host of Israel passed over a stream their leader
noted that the greater number, pausing, stooped
down on their knees and tarried to drink; but
the hardy warriors, eager for the fight, hastily
dipped up the water in their hand, and snatching a
draught passed on. By these did Gideon, the son
of Joash, discomfit the hosts of the Midianites.

The number of the left-handed Benjamites does
not furnish any evidence that this specialty was
more prevalent among them than other tribes.
But it is not difficult to conceive of some resolute
combatant, endowed with the capacity of a leader,
and conscious of his own skill in the use of his
weapons in his dexterous left hand, banding together under his leadership a company selected
on account of their manifesting the same exceptional dexterity. With this as the indispensable
requisite, he was able to muster a body of seven
hundred marksmen, all men of his own tribe, every
one of whom was left-handed, and could sling
stones at a hair's-breadth and not miss. To the
naturally left-handed man such dexterity is in no
degree surprising. Among the instinctively left-
handed, those with whom the bias is slight readily
yield to the influence of example and education,
and so pass over to the majority. Only those in
whom the propensity is too strong to yield to such
influences remain. They are, therefore, exceptionally dexterous with their left hand; and are thus
not only distinguished from the equally expert
right-handed, but are, still more, an exception to
the large majority in whom the bias is so slight,

and the dexterity so partial, that their practice is little more than a compliance with the usage of the majority.

It is important to keep in view the fact that the relative numbers furnished by the narrative in the Book of Judges do not suggest that the tribe of Benjamin differed in the above respect from other tribes. Of twenty-six thousand Benjamites that drew the sword, there were the seven hundred left-handed slingers, or barely 2·7 per cent, which does not greatly differ from the proportion noted at the present time. In the song of triumph for the avenging of Israel over the Canaanites, in the same Book of Judges, the deed of vengeance by which Sisera, the captain of the host of Jabin, King of Canaan, perished by the hand of a woman, is thus celebrated: "She put her hand to the nail, and her right hand to the workman's hammer; and with the hammer she smote Sisera." Here, as we see, while their deliverer from the oppression of the Moabites is noted as a Benjamite, a left-handed man; Jael, the wife of Heber the Kenite, is blessed above women, who with her right hand smote the enemy of God and her people. Along with those references may be noted one of a later date, recorded in the first Book of Chronicles. When David was in hiding from Saul at Ziklag there came to him a company of Saul's brethren of Benjamin, mighty men, armed with bows, who could use both the right hand and the left in hurling stones and shooting arrows out of a bow. These latter, it will be observed, are noted not as left-handed, but ambidextrous; but this is characteristic of all left-handed persons as an inevitable result of education or compliance with the prevailing usage; though even amongst them the unwonted facility with both hands rarely, if ever, entirely supersedes the greater dexterity of the left hand. Possibly the patronymic of the tribe gave significance to such deviations from normal usage; but either for this or some unnoted reason the descendants of Benjamin, the Son of the Right Hand, appear to have obtained notoriety for exceptional aptitude in the use of either hand.

CHAPTER VII

GUIDED by my own personal experience, now extending over a good deal more than threescore and ten years, the Benjamites of Saul's host, who could hurl stones with equal facility by either hand, seem to me greatly more surprising and exceptional than the left-handed company of seven hundred, every one of whom could sling stones at a hair's-breadth and not miss. It is contrary to the nearly universal and almost inevitable preferential use of one hand. It naturally followed on such preference that this unvarying employment led not only to its receiving a distinctive appellation, but that the term so used came to be associated with ideas of dignity, honour, and trust; and as such is perpetuated in the languages both of civilised and savage races. But

this suggests another inquiry of important significance in the determination of the results.   The
application of the Latin *dexter* to " right-handedness "
specifically, as well as to general dexterity in its
more comprehensive sense, points, like the record
of the old Benjamites, to the habitual use of one
hand in preference to the other; but does it necessarily imply that *their* " right hand " was the one
on that side which we now concur in calling
dexter or right?   In the exigencies of war or the
chase, and still more in many of the daily requirements of civilised life, it is necessary that there
should be no hesitation as to which hand shall be
used.   Promptness and dexterity depend on this,
and no hesitation is felt.   But, still further, in many
cases of combined action it is needful that the hand
so used shall be the same; and wherever such a
conformity of practice is recognised the hand so
used, whichever it be, is that on which *dexterity*
depends, and becomes practically the *right* hand.
The term *yamin*, " the right hand," already noted as
the root of the proper name Benjamin, and of the
tribe thus curiously distinguished for its left-handed
warriors and skilled marksmen, is derived from the
verb *yāmăn*, to be firm, to be faithful, as the right

hand is given as a pledge of fidelity, *e.g.* "The Lord
hath sworn by his right hand" (Isa. lxii. 8).
So in the Arabic form, *bimin Allah*, by the right
hand of Allah. So also with the Hebrews and other
ancient nations, as still among ourselves, the seat at
the right hand of the host, or of any dignitary,
was the place of honour; as when Solomon "caused
a seat to be set for the king's mother; and she
sat on his right hand" (1 Kings ii. 19). Again,
the term is frequently used in opposition to *semol*,
left hand; as when the children of Israel would
pass through Edom; "We will go by the king's
high way; we will not turn to the right hand nor
to the left" (Num. xx. 17).

But a further use and significance of the terms
helps us to the fact that the Hebrew *yamin* and
our *right hand* are the same. In its secondary
meaning it signified the "south," as in Ezekiel
xlvii. 1: "The forefront of the house stood toward
the east, and the waters came down from under
from the right side of the house, at the south side
of the altar." The four points are accordingly
expressed thus in Hebrew: *yamin*, the right, the
south; *kedem*, the front, the east; *semol*, the left,
the north; *achor*, behind, the west. To the old

Hebrew, when looking to the east, the west was thus behind, the south on his right hand, and the north on his left. This determination of the right and left in relation to the east is not peculiar to the Hebrews. Many nations appear to have designated the south in the same manner, as being on the right hand when looking to the east. Its origin may be traced with little hesitation to the associations with the most ancient and dignified form of false worship, the paying divine honours to the Sun, as he rises in the east, as the Lord of Day. Thus we find in the Sanskrit *dakshina*, right hand, south ; *puras*, in front, eastward ; *apara*, *paçchima*, behind, west ; *uttara*, northern, to the left. The old Irish has, in like manner, *deas* or *ders*, on the right, southward ; *oirthear*, in front, east ; *jav*, behind, west ; *tuath*, north, from *thuaidh*, left. An analogous practice among the Eskimos, though suggested by a different cause, illustrates a similar origin for the terms "right" and "left." Dr. H. Fink in a communication to the Anthropological Institute (June 1885) remarks : "To indicate the quarters of the globe, the Greenlanders use at once two systems. Besides the ordinary one, they derive another from the view of the open sea, distinguishing what is to

the left and to the right hand. The latter appears
to have been the original method of determining
the bearings, but gradually the words for the left
and the right side came to signify at the same time
' south ' and ' north.' "

A diverse idea is illustrated by the like secondary
significance of the Greek σκαιός, left, or on the left
hand; but also used as " west," or " westward," as
in the *Iliad*, iii. 149, σκαιαὶ πύλαι, the west gate of
Troy. The Greek augur, turning as he did his face
to the north, had the left—the sinister, ill-omened,
unlucky side,—on the west. Hence the metaphorical significance of ἀριστερός, ominous, boding
ill. But the Greeks had also that other mode of
expressing the *right and left* already referred to,
derived from their mode of bearing arms. Ancient
sculpture, the paintings on tombs and fictile ware,
Egyptian, Assyrian, and classic statuary, all illustrate
the methods of carrying the shield, and of wielding
the sword or spear. Hence the shield-hand became
synonymous with the left. The word ἀριστερός
has also been interpreted as " the shield-bearing
arm."

Among the Romans we may trace some survival
of the ancient practice of worshipping towards the

east, as in Livy, i. 18, where the augurs are said
to turn the right side to the south, and the left side
to the north.   But the original significance of
turning to the east had then been lost sight of;
and the particular quarter of the heavens towards
which the Roman augur was to look appears to have
been latterly very much at the will of the augur
himself.   It was, at any rate, variable.   Livy indicates the east, but Varro assigns the south, and
Frontinus the west.   Probably part of the augur's
professional skill consisted in selecting the aspect of
the heavens suited to the occasion.   But this done,
the flight of birds and other appearances on the
right or on the left determined the will of the gods.
" Why," asks Cicero, himself an augur, " why should
the raven on the right and the crow on the left
make a confirmatory augury ? "   " Cur a dextra
corvus, a sinistra cornix faciat ratum ? "   (*De
Divin.* i.)   The left was the side on which the
thunder was declared to be heard which confirmed
the inauguration of a magistrate, and in other
respects the augur regarded it with special awe.
But still the right side was, in all ordinary acceptance, the propitious one, as in the address to
Hercules (*Æn.* viii. 302)—

Salve, vera Jovis proles, pecus addite divis ;
Et nos et tua dexter adi pede sacra secundo.

The traces of a term of common origin for right
(south) in so many of the Indo-European languages
is interesting and suggestive, though the ultimate
word is still open to question.   How the equivalent
terms run through the whole system may be seen
from the following illustrations : Sanskrit, *dakshina*
(cf. *deccan*) ; Zend, *dashina* ; Gothic, *taihs-vo* ; O.H.
German, *zëso* ; Lithuanian, *deszine* ; Gaelic, *dheas* ;
Erse, *dess* (*deas*) ; Latin, *dexter* ; Greek, δεξιός, etc.
The immediate Sanskrit stem *daksh* means " to be
right, or fitting " ; secondarily, " to be dexterous,
clever," etc.   This is evidently from a root *dek*, as
the western languages show.   It was usual at an
earlier period to trace the whole to the root *dik*, to
show, to point ; but this is now given up.   Probably
the Greek δέκ-ομαι (δέχομαι), take, receive, preserves
the original stem, with the idea primarily of " seizing,
catching."   This leads naturally to a comparison of
δάκτ-υ-λος, finger, and *dig-i-tus*, δοκ-ά-νη, fork, etc.
(see Curtius's *Outlines of Greek Etymology*).

Right-handed usages, and the ideas which they
suggest, largely influence the ceremonial customs
of many nations, affect their religious observances,

bear a significant part in the marriage rites, and are interwoven with the most familiar social usages. Among the ancient Greeks the rites of the social board required the passing of the wine from right to left,—or, at any rate, in one invariable direction,—as indicated by Homer in his description of the feast of the gods (*Iliad*, i. 597, θεοῖς ἐνδέξια πᾶσιν οἰνοχόει), where Hephæstus goes round and pours out the sweet nectar to the assembled gods. The direction pursued by the cupbearer would be determined by his bearing the flagon in his right hand, and so walking with his right side towards the guests. This is, indeed, a point of dispute among scholars. But it is not questioned that a uniform practice prevailed, dependent on the recognition of right and left-handedness; and this is no less apparent among the Romans than the Greeks. It is set forth in the most unmusical of Horace's hexameters : " Ille sinistrorsum, hic dextrorsum abit ; " and finds its precise elucidation from many independent sources, in the allusions of the poets, in the works of sculptors, and in the decorations of fictile ware.

CHAPTER VIII

HANDWRITING

IT is manifestly important to determine whether the term used by the Ninevite, the Assyrian, Greek, Roman, and other ancient nations for the right hand was exclusively limited to the member of the body on what is now universally recognised as the right side; or was applicable to either hand, implying no more than the one habitually and preferentially employed. But the true right and left of the Hebrew and other ancient Semitic nations has a special significance, in view of the fact that, whilst the great class of Aryan languages, as well as the Etruscan and others of indeterminate classification, appear, from a remote date, to have been written from left to right; all the Semitic languages, except the Ethiopic, as well as those of other races that have derived

H

their written characters from the Arabian,—such as
the Turks, Malays, and Persians,—are written from
right to left. Habit has so largely modified our
current handwriting, and adapted its characters to
forms best suited for continuous and rapid execution in the one direction, that the reversal of this at
once suggests the idea of a left-handed people. But
the assumption is suggested by a misinterpretation
of the evidence. So long as each character was
separately drawn, and when, moreover, they were
pictorial or ideographic, it was, in reality, more
natural to begin at the right, or nearer side, of the
papyrus or tablet, than to pass over to the left.
The forms of all written characters are largely
affected by their mode of use, as is abundantly
illustrated in the transformation of the Egyptian
ideographs in the later demotic writing. The forms
of the old Semitic alphabet, like the Egyptian hieroglyphics, are specially adapted to cutting on stone.
The square Hebrew characters are of much later
date; but they also, like the uncials of early
Christian manuscripts, were executed singly, and
therefore could be written as easily from right to
left as in a reverse order. The oldest alphabets
indicate a special adaptation for monumental inscrip-

tion. The Runic characters of northern Europe
owe their peculiar form apparently to their being
primarily cut on wood. When papyrus leaves were
substituted for stone, a change was inevitable; but
the direction of the writing only becomes significant
in reference to a current hand. The Greek fashion
of *boustrophedon*, or alternating like the course of
oxen in ploughing, illustrates the natural process
of beginning at the side nearest to the hand; nor
did either this, or the still earlier mode of writing
in columns, as with the ancient Egyptians, or the
Chinese, present any impediment, so long as it was
executed in detached characters. But so soon as
the reed or quill, with the coloured pigment, began
to supersede the chisel, the hieratic writing assumed
a modified form; and when it passed into the later
demotic handwriting, with its seemingly arbitrary
script, the same influences were brought into play
which control the modern penman in the slope,
direction, and force of his stroke. One important
exception, however, still remained. Although, as in
writing Greek, the tendency towards the adoption
of tied letters was inevitable, yet to the last the
enchorial or demotic writing was mainly executed
in detached characters, and does not, therefore, con-

stitute a true current handwriting, such as in our own continuous penmanship leaves no room for doubt as to the hand by which it was executed. Any sufficiently ambidextrous penman, attempting to copy a piece of modern current writing with either hand, would determine beyond all question its right-handed execution.   But no such certain result is found on applying the same test to the Egyptian demotic.   I have tried it on two of the Louvre demotic MSS. and a portion of a Turin papyrus, and find that they can be copied with nearly equal dexterity with either hand.   Some of the characters are more easily and naturally executed, without lifting the pen, with the left hand than the right. Others again, in the slope and the direction of the thickening of the stroke, suggest a right-handed execution ; but habit in the forming of the characters, as in writing Greek or Arabic, would speedily overcome any such difficulty either way.   I feel assured that no habitually left-handed writer would find any difficulty in acquiring the unmodified demotic hand; whereas no amount of dexterity of the penman compelled to resort to his left hand in executing ordinary current writing suffices to prevent such a modification in the slope, the stroke and the formation of the characters, as clearly indicates the change.

Attention has been recently called to this special aspect of the subject in a minutely detailed article in the *Archivio Italiano per le Malatie Nervose*, of September 1890, by Dr. D'Abundo Guiseppe, of the University of Pisa. The inquiry was suggested to the Pisan professor by the peculiar case of a left-handed patient, thus stated by him : " I was treating electrically a gentleman, thirty-three years of age, who had been affected for two years with difficulty in writing, and which proved to be a typical case of the spasm called *writer's cramp*. The fact to which I desire to draw attention is that the gentleman was left-handed, and had been so from his birth, so that he preferentially used the left hand except in writing, as he had learned to write with the right hand. He was a person of good intellect and superior culture ; and he had taught himself to sketch and paint with the left hand. Under the electric treatment he improved, but in view of the liability to relapse, I advised him to commence practising writing with the left hand ; more especially as he is left-handed. But he informed me that in the first attempts made by him he felt, in addition to the

difficulty; that they produced painful sensations in
the right arm, as if he were writing with it. Wish-
ing to master the facts, I caused him to write in
my presence; and I observed that, instead of com-
mencing from left to right, he automatically pro-
ceeded from right to left. At my request, he began
with the greatest readiness and rapidity to write
some lines which I dictated to him. What struck
me was the rapidity with which he wrote, the regu-
larity of the writing, and the ease with which, with
unruled paper, he went on writing from right to left.
He assured me that he had never before made any
attempt to write in that way; and he was himself
really surprised."[1]

Dr. Guiseppe's attention being thus directed to
this aspect of the subject, his next aim was to
determine whether the phenomenon might not be
physiological, and specially characteristic of left-
handed persons; and he naturally reverted to the
pathological evidence bearing on left-handed manifestations. He points out that Buchwald, in three
cases of aphasia, had found a very peculiar disturb-
ance of written language, which consisted in the fact

[1] *Archivio Italiano*, Milan, September 1890, "Su di alcune
particolarità della scrittura dei mancini," p. 298.

that the letters were written by the patient from right
to left, with reverted slope. He accordingly made
further research, with a special view to determine
whether this peculiar manifestation was due to
morbid causes. Unfortunately, although he states
that the subjects of his observation included a considerable number of left-handed persons, the cases
stated by him in detail are mainly those of the
right-handed who, by reason of injury or loss of the
right hand, had been compelled to cultivate the use
of the other. Such cases, however, amount to no
more than evidence of the extent to which the left
hand may be educated, and so made to perform all
the functions of the right hand. To one, indeed,
familiar by practical experience with the exceptional
facilities and the impediments of the left-handed, it
is curious to observe the difficulty experienced by a
highly intelligent scientific student of the phenomena,
to appreciate what seems to the ordinary left-
handed man not only natural but inevitable. In
the case of Dr. Guiseppe's original patient, he wrote
reversely instinctively, and with ease, on the first
attempt to use the unfamiliar pen in his left hand.
Acquired left-handedness revealed itself, on the
contrary, in the writer placing the paper obliquely ;

or in other ways showing that, with all the facility derived from long practice, it was the result of effort and a persevering contest with nature. Dr. Guiseppe accordingly adds in a summary of results: "In general, I have discovered that right-handed persons who became the subjects of disease affecting the right arm from their infancy were forced to learn to write with the left hand; and they wrote from right to left with sufficient facility, varying the slope of the letters. Those, however, who had become affected with disease in the right arm in adult life, when they had already familiarly practised writing with the right hand, and in consequence of disease had been obliged to resort to the left hand, were less successful in writing with the reversed slope."[1]

To the naturally left-handed person, especially when he has enjoyed the unrestrained use of the pencil in his facile hand, the reversed slope is the easiest, and the only natural one. But this is entirely traceable to the comparatively modern element of cursive writing. No such cause affected the graver, or the hieroglyphic depictor of ideographs, even when reduced to their most arbitrary demotic forms, so long as they were executed singly.

[1] *Archivio Italiano*, September 1890, p. 304.

So soon as the habitual use of the papyrus, with
the reed pen and coloured pigments, had developed
any uniformity of usage, the customary method of
writing by the Egyptian appears to have accorded
with that in use among the Hebrew and other
Semitic races; though examples do occur of true
hieroglyphic papyri written from left to right.   But
the pictorial character of such writings furnishes
another test.   It is easier for a right-handed draftsman to draw a profile with the face looking towards
the left; and the same influence might be anticipated to affect the direction of the characters
incised on the walls of temples and palaces.   This
has accordingly suggested an available clue to
Egyptian right or left-handedness.   But the evidence
adduced from Egyptian monuments is liable to
mislead.   A writer in *Nature* (J. S., 14th April
1870) states as the result of a careful survey of
the examples in the British Museum, that the
hieroglyphic profiles there generally look to the
right, and so suggest the work of a left-handed
people.   Other and more suggestive evidence from
the monuments of Egypt points to the same conclusion, but it is deceptive.   The hieroglyphic
sculptures of the Egyptians, like the cufic inscrip-

tions in Arabian architecture, are mainly decorative ;
and are arranged symmetrically for architectural
effect. The same principle regulated their intro-
duction on sarcophagi. Of this, examples in the
British Museum furnish abundant illustration. On
the great sarcophagus of Sebaksi, priest of Phtha,
the profiles on the right and left column look
towards the centre line ; and hence the element
of right-handedness is subordinated to decorative
requirements. If this is overlooked, the left-handedness ascribed above to the ancient Egyptians may
seem to be settled beyond dispute by numerous
representations both of gods and men, engaged in
the actual process of writing. Among the incidents
introduced in the oft-repeated judgment scene of
Osiris,—as on the Adytum of the Temple of Dayr
el Medineh, of which I have a photograph,—Thoth,
the Egyptian God of Letters, stands with the stylus
in his left hand, and a papyrus or tablet in his right,
and records concerning the deceased, in the presence
of the divine judge, the results of the literal weighing in the balance of the deeds done in the body.
In other smaller representations of the same scene,
Thoth is similarly introduced holding the stylus in
his left hand. So also, in the decorations on the

wall of the great chamber in the rock-temple of
Abou Simbel, Rameses is represented slaying his
enemies with a club, which is held in his left hand;
and the goddess Pasht is shown decapitating her
prisoners with a scimitar also in the left hand.
This evidence seems sufficiently direct and indisputable to settle the question; yet further research
leaves no doubt that it is illusory. Ample evidence
to the contrary is to be found in Champollion's
Monuments de l'Egypte et de la Nubie; and is fully
confirmed by Maxime du Camp's *Photographic
Pictures of Egypt, Nubia*, etc., by Sir J. Gardner
Wilkinson's *Manners and Customs of the Ancient
Egyptians*, and by other photographic and pictorial
evidence. In a group, for example, photographed
by Du Camp, from the exterior of the sanctuary of
the palace of Karnac, where the Pharaoh is represented crowned by the ibis and hawk-headed deities,
Thoth and Horus, the hieroglyphics are cut on either
side so as to look towards the central figure. The
same arrangement is repeated in another group at
Ipsamboul, engraved by Champollion, *Monuments de
l'Egypte* (vol. i. Pl. 5). Still more, where figures
are intermingled, looking in opposite directions,—as
shown in a photograph of the elaborately sculptured

posterior façade of the Great Temple of Denderah,—
the accompanying hieroglyphics, graven in column,
vary in direction in accordance with that of the
figure to which they refer.   Columns of hieroglyphics
repeatedly occur, separating the seated deity and a
worshipper standing before him, and only divided by
a perpendicular line, where the characters are turned
in opposite directions corresponding to those of the
immediately adjacent figures.

When, as in the Judgment scene at El Medineh
and elsewhere, Osiris is seated looking to the right,
Thoth faces him, holding in the off-hand—as more
extended, by reason of the simple perspective,—the
papyrus or tablet; while the pen or style is held in
the near or left hand.   To have placed the pen and
tablet in the opposite hands would have required a
complex perspective and foreshortening, or would
have left the whole action obscure and unsuited for
monumental effect.   Nevertheless, the difficulty is
overcome in repeated examples: as in a repetition
of the same scene engraved in Sir J. Gardner
Wilkinson's *Manners and Customs of the Ancient
Egyptians* (Pl. 88), and on a beautifully executed
papyrus, part of *The Book of the Dead*, now in the
Louvre, and reproduced in facsimile in Sylvestre's

Universal Palæography (vol. i. Pl. 46), in both of
which Thoth holds the pen or style in the right
hand. The latter also includes a shearer holding
the sickle in his right hand, and a female sower,
with the seed-basket on her left arm, scattering the
seed with her right hand. Examples of scribes,
stewards, and others engaged in writing, are no less
common in the scenes of ordinary life ; and though
when looking to the left, they are at times represented holding the style or pen in the left hand,
yet the preponderance of evidence suffices to refer
this to the exigencies of primitive perspective. The
steward in a sculptured scene from a tomb at
Elethya (*Monuments de l'Egypte*, Pl. 142) receives
and writes down a report of the cattle from the
field servants, holding the style in his right hand
and the tablet in his left. So is it with the registrar
and the scribes (Wilkinson, Figs. 85, 86), the
steward who takes account of the grain delivered
(Fig. 387), and the notary and scribes (Figs. 73,
78)—all from Thebes, where they superintend the
weighing at the public scales, and enumerate a group
of negro slaves.

In the colossal sculptures on the façades of the
great temples, where complex perspective and fore-

shortening would interfere with the architectural effect, the hand in which the mace or weapon is held appears to be mainly determined by the direction to which the figure looks. At Ipsamboul, as shown in *Monuments de l'Egypte,* Pl. 11, Rameses grasps with his right hand, by the hair of the head, a group of captives of various races, negroes included, while he smites them with a scimitar or pole-axe, wielded in his left hand; but an onlooker, turned in the opposite direction, holds the sword in his right hand. This transposition is more markedly shown in two scenes from the same temple (Pl. 28). In the one Rameses, looking to the right, wields the pole-axe in the near or right hand, as he smites a kneeling Asiatic; in the other, where he looks to the left, he holds his weapon again in the near, but now the left hand, as he smites a kneeling negro. On the same temple soldiers are represented holding spears in the near hand, right or left, according to the direction they are looking (Pl. 22); and swords and shields are transposed in like manner (Pl. 28). The same is seen in the siege scenes and military reviews of Rameses the Great, on the walls of Thebes and elsewhere. The evidence is misleading if the primary aim of architectural decoration is not kept

in view. In an example from Karnac—appealed
to in proof that the Egyptians were a left-handed
people,—where Thotmes III. holds his offering in
the extended left hand, his right side is stated to
be towards the observer. Nor are similar examples
rare. Thoth and other deities, sculptured in colossal
proportions, on the Grand Temple of Isis, at Philæ,
as shown by Du Camp, in like manner have their
right sides towards the observer, and hold each the
mace or sceptre in the extended left hand. But on
turning to the photographs of the Great Temple of
Denderah, where another colossal series of deities
is represented in precisely the same attitude, but
looking in the opposite direction, the official symbols
are reversed, and each holds the sceptre in the
extended right hand. Numerous similar instances
are given by Wilkinson; as in the dedication of
the pylon of a temple to Amun by Rameses III.,
Thebes (No. 470); the Goddesses of the West and
East, looking in corresponding directions (No. 461),
etc.

Examples, however, occur where the conventional
formulæ of Egyptian sculpture have been abandoned,
and the artist has overcome the difficulties of perspective; as in a remarkable scene in the Mem-

monium, at Thebes, where Atmoo, Thoth, and a female (styled by Wilkinson the Goddess of Letters) are all engaged in writing the name of Rameses on the fruit of the Persea tree. Though looking in opposite directions, each holds the pen in the right hand (Wilkinson, Pl. 54 A). So also at Beni Hassan, two artists kneeling in front of a board, face each other, and each paints an animal, holding the brush in the right hand. At Medinet Habou, Thebes, more than one scene of draught-players occurs, where the players, facing each other, each hold the piece in the right hand. Similar illustrations repeatedly occur.

Among another people, of kindred artistic skill, whose records have been brought anew to light in recent years, their monumental evidence appears to furnish more definite results ; while the curiously definite reference in the Book of Jonah leaves no room to doubt that among the ancient Ninevites it was recognised that at the earliest stage when voluntary action co-operated with the rational will, a specific hand was habitually in use. That the ancient dwellers on the Euphrates and the Tigris were a right-handed people appears to be borne out by their elaborate sculpture, recovered at Kourjunjik, Khorsabad, Nimroud, and other buried cities of the great plain. The sculptures are in relief, and frequently of a less conventional character than those of the Egyptian monuments, and are consequently less affected by the aspect and position of the figures. The gigantic figure of the Assyrian Hercules—or, as supposed, of the mighty hunter Nimrod,—found between the winged bulls, in the great court of the Palace of Khorsabad, is represented strangling a young lion, which he presses against his chest with his left arm, while he holds in his right hand a weapon of the chase, supposed to be analogous to the Australian boomerang. On the walls of the same palace the great king appears with his staff in his right hand, while his left hand rests on the pommel of his sword. Behind him a eunuch holds in his right hand, over the king's head, a fan or fly-flapper ; and so with other officers in attendance. Soldiers bear their swords and axes in the right hand, and their shields on the left arm. A prisoner is being flayed alive by an operator who holds the knife in the right hand. The king himself puts out the eyes of another captive, holding the spear in his right hand, while he retains in his left the end of a cord attached to his victim. Similar evi-

dence abounds throughout the elaborate series of
sculptures in the British Museum and in the Louvre.
Everywhere gods and men are represented as " dis-
cerning between their right hand and their left," and
giving the preference to the former.

It has been already shown that in languages of
the American continent, as in those of the Algon-
quins and the Iroquois, the recognition of the distinction between the right and left hand is apparent; and on turning to the monuments of a native
American civilisation, evidence similar to that
derived from the sculptures of Egypt and Assyria
serves to show that the same hand had the preference in the New World as in the Old. In the
Palenque hieroglyphics of Central America, for
example, in which human and animal heads frequently occur among the sculptured characters, it
is noticeable that they invariably look towards the
left, indicating, as it appears to me, that they are
the graven inscriptions of a lettered people who
were accustomed to write the same characters from
left to right on paper or skins. Indeed, the pictorial
groups on the Copan statues seem to be the true
hieroglyphic characters; while the Palenque inscriptions correspond to the abbreviated hieratic

writing. The direction of the profile was a matter
of no moment to the sculptor, but if the scribe held
his pen or style in his right hand, like the modern
clerk, he would as naturally draw the left profile as
the penman slopes his current hand to the right.
In the pictorial hieroglyphics, reproduced in Lord
Kingsborough's *Mexican Antiquities*, as in other
illustrations of the arts of Mexico and Central
America, it is also apparent that the battle-axe and
other weapons and implements are most frequently
held in the right hand. But to this exceptions
occur; and it is obvious that there also the crude
perspective of the artist influenced the disposition
of the tools, or weapons, according to the action
designed to be represented, and the direction in
which the actor looked. Such are some of the
indications which seem to point to a uniform usage,
in so far as we can recover evidence of the practice
among ancient nations; while far behind their
most venerable records lie the chronicles of palæolithic ages: of the men of the drift and of the
caves of Europe's prehistoric dawn.

So far, then, it seems to be proved that not only
among cultured and civilised races, but among the
barbarous tribes of both hemispheres,—in Australia,

Polynesia, among the Arctic tribes of our northern hemisphere at the present day, and among the palæolithic men of Europe's post-pliocene times,— not only has a habitual preference been manifested for the use of one hand rather than the other, but among all alike the same hand has been preferred. Yet, also, it is no less noteworthy that this prevailing uniformity of practice has always been accompanied by some very pronounced exceptions. Not only are cases of exceptional facility in the use of both hands of frequent occurrence, but while right-handed-ness everywhere predominates, left-handedness is nowhere unknown. The skill of the combatant in hitting with both hands is indeed a favourite topic of poetic laudation, though this is characteristic of every well-trained boxer. In the combat between Entellus and Dares (*Æn.* v. 456), the passionate Entellus strikes now with his right hand and again with his left—

> Præcipitemque Daren ardens agit æquore toto,
> Nunc dextra ingeminans ictus, nunc ille sinistra.

But the more general duty assigned to the left hand is as the guard or the shield-bearer, as where Æneas gives the signal to his comrades, in sight of the Trojans (*Æn.* x. 261)—

Stans celsa in puppi ; clipeum cum deinde sinistra
Extulit ardentem.

The right hand may be said to express all active
volition and all beneficent action, as in *Æn.* vi. 370,
" Da dextram misero," " Give thy right hand to the
wretched," *i.e.* give him aid ; and so in many other
examples, all indicative of right-handedness as the
rule. The only exception I have been able to
discover occurs in a curious passage in the *Eclogues*
of Stobæus Περὶ ψυχῆς, in a dialogue between
Horus and Isis, where, after describing a variety of
races of men, and their peculiarities, it thus proceeds :
" An indication of this is found in the circumstance
that southern races, that is, those who dwell on the
earth's summit, have fine heads and good hair ;
eastern races are prompt to battle, and skilled in
archery, for the right hand is the seat of these
qualities. Western races are cautious, and for the
most part left-handed ; and whilst the activity which
other men display belongs to their right side, these
races favour the left." Stobæus, the Macedonian,
belongs, at earliest, to the end of the fifth century
of our era, but he collected diligently from numerous
ancient authors, some of whom would otherwise be
unknown ; but the passage is part of a description in

which he speaks of the earth as having its apex or
head to the south, the right shoulder to the east, and
the left to the south-west ; and the left-handed races
of the west may be so merely in a figurative sense.
This description, at any rate, is the only indication,
vague and dubious as it is, of a belief in the existence
of a left-handed race.

Thus all evidence appears to conflict with the
idea that the preferential employment of one hand
can be accounted for by a mere general compliance
with prevailing custom.   Everywhere, in all ages,
and in the most diverse conditions of civilised and
savage life, the predominant usage is the same.   Not
that there are not everywhere marked exceptions to
the prevailing practice, in left-handed athletes, handi-
craftsmen, artificers, and artists, generally characterised by unusual dexterity ; but the farther research
is carried, it becomes the more apparent that these
are exceptional deviations from the normal usage of
humanity.

CHAPTER IX

PSYCHO-PHYSICAL ACTION

THE venerable philosopher of Chelsea, musing, with sorrowful experiences to stimulate inquisitiveness, after wondering if any people are to be found barbarous enough not to have this distinction of hands, sums up with the evasion: "Why that particular hand was chosen is a question not to be settled; not worth asking except as a kind of riddle." It seems, however, to be regarded by intelligent inquirers as a riddle that ought to be, and that can be solved, though they have wandered into very diverse courses in search of a solution.

It has been affirmed, for example, that while the right hand is more sensitive to touch, and, as it were, the special seat of the sense of feeling,—as with the right-handed it may well be from constant employment in all operations involving such a test, —the left hand is stated to be the more sensitive to any change of temperature.

Mr. George Henry Lewes, in his *Physiology of Common Life*, says : " If the two hands be dipped in two basins of water at the same temperature, the left hand will feel the greater sensation of warmth ; nay, it will do this even where the thermometers show that the water in the left basin is really somewhat colder than in the right basin ; " and he adds : " I suspect that with ' left-handed ' persons the reverse would be found." On the assumption that the former is a well-established law, the latter seems a legitimate inference ; but, as will be seen from what follows, there is good reason for doubting that the statement rests on an adequate amount of evidence.

To determine the prevalence of this relative sensitiveness to heat of the right and left hand, the test ought to be applied to uncultured and savage, as well as to civilised man. The elements which tend to complicate the inquiry are very various. The left-handed man is nearly always ambidextrous, though with an instinctive preference for the left hand in any operation requiring either special dexterity or unusual force. Hence his right hand,

though less in use than that of the right-handed
man, is in no such condition of habitual inertia as
the other's left hand. Again, a large number give
the preference to the right hand from a mere compliance with the practice of the majority ; but with
no special innate impulse to the use of one hand
rather than the other. But besides those, there is
a considerable minority in whom certain indications
suffice to show that the bias, though no strong and
overruling impulse, is in favour of the left hand.
I have, accordingly, had a series of tentative observations made for me in the Physical Laboratory
of the University of Toronto, under the super-
intendence of Mr. W. J. Loudon, Demonstrator of
Physics. The undergraduates willingly submitted
themselves to the requisite tests ; and the series of
experiments were carried out by Mr. Loudon with
the utmost care. No idea was allowed to transpire
calculated to suggest anticipated results. A highly
characteristic Canadian test of any latent tendency
to right or left-handedness was employed. In the
use of the axe, so familiar to nearly every Canadian,
alike in summer camping-out and in the prepara-
tion of winter fuel, the instinctive preference for
one or other hand is shown in always keeping the

surer hand nearest the axe-blade.   This test was
the one appealed to in classifying those who submitted to the following experiments.   The trial was
made with water very nearly 30° centigrade.   The
results arrived at are shown here, the persons
experimented on being divided into three classes :
(1) Right-handed, or those who habitually use the
right hand, and who in handling an axe place the
right hand above the left, nearest the axe-head.
(2) Ordinarily using the right hand, but placing
the left hand above the right in the use of the
axe.   These appear to be generally ambidextrous.
(3) Those who are generally said to be left-handed,
but employ the pen in the right hand, and also use
that hand in many other operations.   This class
includes very varying degrees of bias ; and though
loosely characterised as left-handed, from some
greater or less tendency to use that hand, the majority of them were found to place the right hand
above the left in the use of the axe.   One hundred
and sixty-four in all were subjected to the test, with
the following results : Of ninety right-handed
persons, thirty-five found the right hand the more
sensitive, thirty-three the left hand, and twenty-two
failed to discern an appreciable difference.   Of fifty-

six persons of the second class, right-handed but using the left as the guiding hand with the axe, seventeen found the right hand the more sensitive, and fifteen the left, while twenty-four felt no difference. Of eighteen of the third class, six found the right hand the more sensitive, seven the left hand, and five could detect no difference. Another case was that of a lady, decidedly left-handed, who writes, sews, and apparently does nearly everything with her left hand. She tried at three temperatures, viz. 5°, 30°, and 48° centigrade. In the first case she pronounced the left hand to be undoubtedly colder, in the second she observed no difference, and in the third, the left hand was undoubtedly warmer. Another lady, also habitually using her needle in the left hand, and otherwise instinctively reverting to that hand in all operations requiring delicate or skilful manipulation, repeated the same experiment more than once at my request; but could not detect any difference in the sensitiveness of either hand. The results thus stated were all arrived at with great care. It is manifest that they fail to confirm the statement set forth in the *Physiology of Common Life*, or to point to any uniformity in the relative sensitiveness of the right and left hands. In so far as either hand may prove to be more sensitive to heat than the other, it is probably due to the constant exertion of the one hand rendering it less sensitive to changes of temperature. Yet even this is doubtful. Two carpenters chanced to be at work in the College building while the above experiments were in progress. They were both right-handed workmen; yet, contrary to expectation, on being subjected to the test, they both pronounced the right hand to be more sensitive to heat. The statement of Mr. Lewes is so definite that the subject may be deserving of more extended experiment under other conditions. Any widely manifested difference in the sensitiveness of one of the hands, apart from its habitual use in all ordinary manipulation, and especially among uncultured races, would assuredly seem to indicate some congenital distinction leading to the preferential use of the right hand. But whatever may be the source of this preference, the difference between the two hands is not so great as to defy the influence of education; as is seen in the case of those who, even late in life, through any injury or loss of the right hand, have been compelled to resort to the less dexterous one.

Of the occurrence of individual examples of left-
handedness the proofs are ample, seemingly from
earliest glimpses of life to the present time; and it
would even appear that, in so far as the small yet
definite amount of evidence of the relative percentage
of the left-handed enables us to judge, it differs little
now from what it did at the dawn of definite history.

Professor Hyrtl of Vienna affirms its prevalence
among the civilised races of Europe in the ratio of
only two per cent; and the number of the old
Benjamite left-handed slingers, as distinguished from
other members of the band of twenty-six thousand
warriors, did not greatly exceed this. In the ruder
conditions of society, where combined action is rare,
and social habits are less binding, a larger number
of exceptions to the prevailing usage may be looked
for; as the tendency of a high civilisation must be
to diminish its manifestation. But education is
powerless to eradicate it where it is strongly manifested in early life. My attention has been long
familiarly directed to it from being myself naturally
left-handed; and the experience of considerably
more than half a century enables me to controvert
the common belief, on which Dr. Humphry founds
the deduction that the superiority of the right hand

is not congenital, but acquired, viz. that " the left
hand may be trained to as great expertness and
strength as the right." On the contrary, my experience accords with that of others in whom inveterate
left-handedness exists, in showing the education of
a lifetime contending with only partial success to
overcome an instinctive natural preference. The
result has been, as in all similar cases, to make
me ambidextrous, yet not strictly speaking ambi-
dexterous.

The importance of this in reference to the
question of the source of right-handedness is obvious.
Mr. James Shaw, by whom the subject has been
brought under the notice of the British Association
and the Anthropological Institute, remarks in a
communication to the latter : " Left-handedness is
very mysterious. It seems to set itself quite against
physiological deductions, and the whole tendency of
art and fashion." Dr. John Evans, when commenting
on this, and on another paper on " Left-handedness "
by Dr. Muirhead, expressed his belief that " the
habit of using the left hand in preference to the
right, though possibly to some extent connected with
the greater supply of blood to one side than the
other, is more often the result of the manner in

which the individual has been carried in infancy."
This reason has been frequently suggested; but if
there were any force in it, the results to be looked
for would rather be an alternation of hands from
generation to generation. The nurse naturally
carries the child on the left arm, with its right side
toward her breast. All objects presented to it are
thus offered to the free left hand; and it is accordingly no uncommon remark that all children are at
first left-handed. If their training while in the
nurse's arms could determine the habit, such is its
undoubted tendency; but if so, the left-handed
nurses of the next generation would reverse the
process.

While, however, right-handedness is no mere
acquired habit, but traceable to specific organic
structure, the opinion has been already expressed
that it is only in a limited number of cases that it
is strongly manifested.

The conclusion I am led to, as the result of long
observation, is that the preferential use of the right
hand is natural and instinctive with some persons;
that with a smaller number an equally strong impulse is felt prompting to the use of the left hand;
but that with the great majority right-handedness

is largely the result of education.   If children are
watched in the nursery, it will be found that the
left hand is offered little less freely than the right.
The nurse or mother is constantly transferring the
spoon from the left to the right hand, correcting the
defective courtesy of the proffered left hand, and in
all ways superinducing right-handedness as a habit.
But wherever the organic structure is well developed
the instinctive preference manifests itself at a very
early stage, and in the case either of decided right-
handedness or left-handedness, it matures into a
determinate law of action, which education may
modify but cannot eradicate.

My colleague, Professor James Mark Baldwin,
has followed up my own researches by instituting
a systematic series of experiments on his infant
daughter, extending over nearly the whole of her
first year, with a view to ascertaining definitely the
time at which the child begins to manifest any
marked preference for either hand.   As a specialist
in the department of psycho-physics, he carried his
inductive research beyond the range embraced in
the present treatise ; dealing with the question of
feelings of efferent nervous discharge or innervation,
the motor force of memories of effortless movement,

and other conceptions of the psychologist which lie
outside of the simpler issue under consideration
here.   Yet they naturally follow from it; for so
soon as volition comes into conscious play, and the
hand obeys the mind, and becomes an organ of the
will, the psychical element is felt to dominate over
the physical; including that very force of will which
aims at eradicating the exceptional left-handedness,
and enforcing an undeviating submission to the law
of the majority.

It is unquestionably of first interest to the
psychologist to inquire not only why the child,
at the early stage in which a choice of hands is
manifested, should prefer the right hand for all
strong movements; but also, whether previous experiences in the use of both hands leave behind a
sense that the nervous discharge which actuated
the right hand was stronger than that which
actuated the left.   But the point aimed at here
is to ascertain the originating physical initiative
of determinate action, antecedent to all memory;
the precursor of any such action stimulated by
memory of an efferent current of discharge of
nervous force.   For that end the following results,
derived from a careful series of observations on the

voluntary actions of a healthy child throughout its first year, are of practical significance and value.

" (1) No trace of preference for either hand was found so long as there were no violent muscular exertions made (based on 2187 systematic experiments in cases of free movement of hands near the body: *i.e.* right hand 585 cases, left hand 568 cases: a difference of 17 cases; both hands 1034 cases; the difference of 17 cases being too slight to have meaning).

" (2) Under the same conditions, the tendency to use both hands together was about double the tendency to use either (seen from the number of cases of the use of both hands in the statistics given above), the period covered being from the child's sixth to her tenth month inclusive.

" (3) A distinct preference for the right hand in violent efforts in reaching became noticeable in the seventh and eighth months. Experiments during the eighth month on this cue gave, in 80 cases, right hand 74 cases, left hand 5 cases, both hands 1 case. In many cases the left hand followed slowly upon the lead of the right. Under the stimulus of bright colours, from 86 cases, 84 were right-hand cases, and 2 left-hand. Right-handed-

ness had accordingly developed under pressure of
muscular effort.

"(4) Up to this time the child had not learned
to stand or to creep; hence the development of one
hand more than the other is not due to differences
in weight between the two longitudinal halves of
the body. As she had not learned to speak, or to
utter articulate sounds with much distinctness, we
may say also that right or left-handedness may
develop while the motor speech centre is not yet
functioning."[1]

But memory of prior experiences, habit confirmed
by persistent usage, and the influence of example
and education, all come into play at an early stage,
and lend confirmation to the natural bias. The
potency of such combined influences must largely
affect the results in many cases where the difference
in force between the two cerebral hemispheres is
slight; and the stimulus to preferential action is
consequently weak, as in many cases it undoubtedly
is, and therefore not calculated to present any insur-
mountable resistance to counteracting or opposing
influences. Under the term education, as a factor
developing or counteracting the weak tendency

[1] *Science*, vol. xvi. pp. 247, 248.

towards either bias, must be included many habits superinduced not only by the example of the majority, but by their constructive appliances. So soon as the child is old enough to be affected by such influences, the fastening of its clothes, the handling of knife and spoon, and of other objects in daily use, help to confirm the habit, until the art of penmanship is mastered, and with this crowning accomplishment—except in cases of strongly marked bias in an opposite direction,—the left hand is relegated to its subordinate place as a supplementary organ, to be called into use when the privileged member finds occasion for its aid.

But on the other hand, an exaggerated estimate is formed of the difficulties experienced by a left-handed person in many of the ordinary actions of life. It is noted by Mr. James Shaw that the buttons of our dress, and the hooks and eyes of all female attire, are expressly adapted to the right hand. Again, Sir Charles Bell remarks: " We think we may conclude that, everything being adapted, in the conveniences of life, to the right hand, as, for example, the direction of the worm of the screw, or of the cutting end of the auger, is not arbitrary, but is related to a natural endowment

of the body.   He who is left-handed is most sensible
to the advantages of this adaptation, from the opening of the parlour door, to the opening of a. penknife." This idea, though widely entertained, is to
a large extent founded on misapprehension. It is
undoubtedly true that the habitual use of the right
hand has controlled the form of many implements,
and influenced the arrangements of dress, as well as
the social customs of society. The musket is fitted
for an habitually right-handed people. So, in like
manner, the adze, the plane, the gimlet, the screw,
and other mechanical tools, must be adapted to one
or the other hand. Scissors, snuffers, shears, and
other implements specially requiring the action of the
thumb and fingers, are all made for the right hand.
So also is it with the scythe of the reaper. Not
only the lock of the gun or rifle, but the bayonet
and the cartridge-pouch, are made or fitted on the
assumption of the right hand being used ; and even
many arrangements of the fastenings of the dress are
adapted to this habitual preference of the one hand
over the other, so that the reversing of button and
button-hole, or hook and eye, is attended with marked
inconvenience. Yet even in this, much of what is
due to habit is ascribed to nature. A Canadian

friend, familiar in his own earlier years, at an English public school and university, with the game of cricket, tells me that when it was introduced for the first time into Canada within the last forty years, left-handed batters were common in every field; but the immigration of English cricketers has since led, for the most part, to the prevailing usage of the mother country. It was not that the batters were, as a rule, left-handed, but that the habit of using the bat on one side or other was, in the majority of cases, so little influenced by any predisposing bias, that it was readily acquired in either way. But, giving full weight to all that has been stated here as to right-handed implements, what are the legitimate conclusions which it teaches? No doubt an habitually left-handed people would have reversed all this. But if, with adze, plane, gimlet, and screw, scythe, reaping-hook, scissors and snuffers, rifle, bayonet, and all else— even to the handle of the parlour door, and the hooks and buttons of his dress,—daily enforcing on the left-handed man a preference for the right hand, he nevertheless persistently adheres to the left hand, the cause of this must lie deeper than a mere habit induced in the nursery.

It is a misapprehension, however, to suppose
that the left-handed man labours under any
conscious disadvantage from the impediments thus
created by the usage of the majority. With rare
exceptions, habit so entirely accustoms him to the
requisite action, that he would be no less put out
by the sudden reversal of the door-handle, knife-
blade, or screw, or the transposition of the buttons
on his dress, than the right-handed man. Habit is
constantly mistaken for nature. The laws of the
road, for example, so universally recognised in
England, have become to all as it were a second
nature; and, as the old rhyme says—

> If you go to the left, you are sure to go right ;
> If you go to the right, you go wrong.

But throughout Canada and the United States the
reverse is the law; and the new immigrant,
adhering to the usage of the mother country, is
sorely perplexed by the persistent wrong-headedness,
as it seems, of every one but himself.

Yet the predominant practice does impress itself
on some few implements in a way sufficiently
marked to remind the left-handed operator that he
is transgressing normal usage. The candle, "our
peculiar and household planet!" as Charles Lamb

designates it, has wellnigh become a thing of the
past; but in the old days of candle-light the
snuffers were among the most unmanageable of
domestic implements to a left-handed man.   They
are so peculiarly adapted to the right hand that the
impediment can only be overcome by the dexterous
shift of inserting the left thumb and finger below
instead of above.   As to the right-handed adaptation of scissors, it is admitted by others, but I am
unconscious of any difficulty that their alteration
would remove.   To Carlyle, as already noted, with
his early experiences of country life, the idea of
right and left-handed mowers attempting to co-
operate presented "the simplest form of an impossibility, which but for the distinction of a 'right
hand,' would have pervaded all human things."
But, although the mower's scythe must be used in a
direction in which the left hand is placed at some
disadvantage—and a left-handed race of mowers
would undoubtedly reverse the scythe—yet even in
this the chief impediment is to co-operation.   The
difficulty to himself is surmountable.   It is his
fellow-workers who are troubled by his operations.
Like the handling of the oar, or still more the
paddle of a canoe, or the use of the musket or

rifle,—so obviously designed for a right-handed
marksman,—the difficulty is soon overcome.   It is
not uncommon to find a left-handed soldier placed
on the left of his company when firing; and an
opportunity—hereafter referred to,—has happily
presented itself for determining the cerebral char-
acteristics which accompany this strongly-marked
type of left-handedness.   As himself incorrigibly
left-handed, the author's own experience in drilling
as a volunteer was that, after a little practice, he
had no difficulty in firing from the right shoulder;
but he never could acquire an equal facility with
his companions in unfixing the bayonet and re-
turning it to its sheath.

But as certain weapons and implements, like
the rifle and the scythe, are specially adapted for
the prevailing right hand, and some ancient implements have been recovered in confirmation of the
antiquity of the bias; so the inveterate left-handed
manipulator at times reinstates himself on an
equality with rival workmen who have thus placed
him at a disadvantage.   Probably the most ancient
example of an implement expressly adapted for the
right hand is the handle of a bronze sickle, found
in 1873 at the lake-dwelling of Möringen, on the

Lake of Brienne, Switzerland. Bronze sickles have long been familiar to the archæologist, among the relics of the prehistoric era known as the Bronze Age; and their forms are included among the illustrations of Dr. Ferdinand Keller's *Lake Dwellings*. But the one now referred to is the first example that has been recovered showing the complete hafted implement. The handle is of yew, and is ingeniously carved so as to lie obliquely to the blade, and allow of its use close to the ground. It is a right-handed implement, carefully fashioned so as to adapt it to the grasp of a very small hand; and is more incapable of use by a left-handed shearer than a mower's scythe. Its peculiar form is shown in an illustration which accompanies Dr. Keller's account; and in noting that the handle is designed for a right-handed person, he adds: " Even in the Stone Age, it has already been noticed that the implements in use at that time were fitted for the right hand only." But if so, the same adaptability was available for the left-handed workman, wherever no necessity for co-operation required him to conform to the usage of the majority. Instances of left-handed carpenters who have provided themselves with benches adapted to their special use

HANDLE OF BRONZE SICKLE, MÖRINGEN, SWITZERLAND.

To face page 138.

have come under my notice. I am also told of a scythe fitted to the requirements of a left-handed mower, who must have been content to work alone; and reference has already been made to sets of golfing drivers and clubs for the convenience of left-handed golfers.

The truly left-handed, equally with the larger percentage of those who may be designated truly right-handed, are exceptionally dexterous; and to the former the idea that the instinctive impulse which influences their preference is a mere acquired habit, traceable mainly to some such bias as the mode of carrying in the nurse's arms in infancy, is utterly untenable. The value of personal experience in determining some of the special points involved in this inquiry is obvious, and will excuse a reference to my own observations, as confirmed by a comparison with those of others equally affected, such as Professor Edward S. Morse, Dr. R. A. Reeve, a former pupil of my own, and my friend, Dr. John Rae, the Arctic explorer. The last remarked in a letter to me, confirming the idea of hereditary transmission: " Your case as to left-handedness seems very like my own. My mother was left-handed, and very neat-handed also. My father had a crooked little

finger on the left hand. So have I." Referring
to personal experience, I may note as common to
myself with other thoroughly left-handed persons,
that, with an instinctive preference for the left hand,
which equally resisted remonstrance, proffered re-
wards, and coercion, I nevertheless learned to use
the pen in the right hand, apparently with no
greater effort than other boys who pass through the
preliminary stages of the art of penmanship. In
this way the right hand was thoroughly educated,
but the preferential instinct remained. The slate-
pencil, the chalk, and penknife were still invariably
used in the left hand, in spite of much opposition
on the part of teachers ; and in later years, when
a taste for drawing has been cultivated with some
degree of success, the pencil and brush are nearly
always used in the left hand. At a comparatively
early age the awkwardness of using the spoon and
knife at table in the left hand was perceived and
overcome. Yet even now, when much fatigued, or
on occasion of unusual difficulty in carving a joint,
the knife is instinctively transferred to the left
hand. Alike in every case where unusual force is
required, as in driving a large nail, wielding a heavy
tool, or striking a blow with the fist, as well as in

any operation demanding special delicacy, the left
hand is employed.   Thus, for example, though the
pen is invariably used in the right hand in penmanship, the crow-quill and etching needle are no
less uniformly employed in the left hand.   Hence,
accordingly, on proceeding to apply the test of the
hand to the demotic writing of the Egyptians, by
copying rapidly the Turin enchorial papyrus already
referred to, first with the right hand and then with
the left, while some of the characters were more
accurately rendered as to slope, thickening of lines,
and curve, with the one hand, and some with the
other, I found it difficult to decide on the whole
which hand executed the transcription with greater
ease.   In proof of the general facility thus acquired,
I may add that I find no difficulty in drawing at
the same time with a pencil in each hand, profiles
of men or animals facing each other.   The attempt
to draw different objects, as a dog's head with the
one hand and a human profile with the other, is
unsuccessful, owing to the complex mental operation
involved ; and in this case the co-operation is apt to
be between the mind and the more facile hand.   In
the simultaneous drawing of reverse profiles there is
what, to an ordinary observer, would appear to be

thorough ambidexterity. Nevertheless, while there
is in such cases of ambidexterity, characteristic of
most left-handed persons, little less command of the
right hand than in those exclusively right-handed,
it is wholly acquired; nor, in my own experience,
has the habit, fostered by the practice of upwards
of seventy years, overcome the preferential use of
the other hand.

When attending the meeting of the American
Association for the Advancement of Science held at
Buffalo in 1867, my attention was attracted by the
facility with which Professor Edward S. Morse used
his left hand when illustrating his communications
by crayon drawings on the blackboard. His ability
in thus appealing to the eye is well known. The
Boston *Evening Transcript*, in commenting on a
course of lectures delivered there, thus proceeds :
" We must not omit to mention the wonderful skill
displayed by Professor Morse in his blackboard
drawings of illustrations, using either hand with
facility, but working chiefly with the left hand.
The rapidity, simplicity, and remarkable finish of
these drawings elicited the heartiest applause of his
audience." Referring to the narrative of my own
experience as a naturally left-handed person subjected

to the usual right-hand training with pen, pencil,
knife, etc., Professor Morse remarks in a letter to
me : " I was particularly struck by the description
of your experiences in the matter, for they so closely
accord with my own : my teachers having in vain
endeavoured to break off the use of the left hand,
which only resulted in teaching me to use my right
hand also.   At a short distance, I can toss or throw
with the right hand quite as accurately as I can with
my left.   But when it comes to flinging a stone or
other object a long distance, I always use the left hand
as coming the most natural.   There are two things
which I cannot possibly do with my right hand,
and that is to drive a nail, or to carve, cut, or
whittle.   For several years I followed the occupation of mechanical draughtsman, and I may say
that there was absolutely no preference in the use
of either hand ; and in marking labels, or lettering
a plan, one hand was just as correct as the other."
I may add here that in my own case, though
habitually using the pen in my right hand, yet
when correcting a proof, or engaged in other dis-
connected writing, especially if using a pencil, I am
apt to resort to the left hand without being conscious
of the change.   In drawing I rarely use the right

hand, and for any specially delicate piece of work,
should find it inadequate to the task.

The same facility is illustrated in the varying
caligraphy of a letter of Professor Morse, in which
he furnished me with the best practical illustration
of the ambidextrous skill so frequently acquired by
the left-handed. He thus writes : " You will observe
that the first page is written with the right hand,
the upper third of this page with the left hand, the
usual way [but with reversed slope], the middle
third of the page with the left hand, reversed [*i.e.*
from right to left], and now I am again writing
with the right hand. As I have habitually used
the right hand in writing, I write more rapidly than
with the other." In the case of Professor Morse,
I may add, the indications of hereditary transmission of left-handedness nearly correspond with
my own. His maternal uncle, and also a cousin,
are left-handed. In my case, the same habit
appeared in a paternal uncle and a niece ; and my
grandson manifested at an early age a decided
preference for the left hand. Even in the absence
of such habitual use of both hands as Professor
Morse practises, the command of the left hand in
the case of a left-handed person is such that very

slight effort is necessary to enable him to use the
pen freely with it.   An apt illustration of this has
been communicated to me by the manager of one of
the Canadian banks.   He had occasion to complain
of the letters of one of his local agents as at times
troublesome to decipher, and instructed him in
certain cases to dictate to a junior clerk who wrote
a clear, legible hand.   The letters subsequently sent
to the manager, though transmitted to him by the
same agent, presented in signature, as in all else, a
totally different caligraphy.   The change of signature
led to inquiry ; when it turned out that his correspondent was left-handed, and by merely shifting
the pen to the more dexterous hand, he was able,
with a very little practice, to substitute for the old
cramped penmanship an upright, rounded, neat, and
very legible handwriting.

In reference to the question of hereditary transmission, the evidence, as in the case of Dr. Rae, is
undoubted.   Dr. R. A. Reeve, in whom also the
original left-handedness has given place to a nearly
equal facility with both hands, informs me that his
father was left-handed. Again Dr. Pye-Smith quotes
from the *Lancet* of October 1870 the case of Mr.
R. A. Lithgow, who writes to say that he himself,

L

his father, and his grandfather have all been left-handed.   This accords with the statement of M. Ribot in his *Heredity*.   " There are," he says, " families in which the special use of the left hand is hereditary.   Girou mentions a family in which the father, the children, and most of the grand-children were left-handed. One of the latter betrayed its left-handedness from earliest infancy, nor could it be broken off the habit, though the left hand was bound and swathed." Such persistent left-handedness is not, indeed, rare.   In an instance communicated to me, both of the parents of a gentleman in Shrop-shire were left-handed.   His mother, accordingly, watched his early manifestations of the same tendency, and employed every available means to counteract it. His left hand was bound up or tied behind him ; and this was persevered in until it was feared that the left arm had been permanently injured. Yet all proved vain.   The boy resumed the use of the left hand as soon as the restraint was removed; and though learning like others to use his right hand with facility in the use of the pen, and in other cases in which custom enforces compliance with the practice of the majority, he remained inveterately left-handed. Again a Canadian friend, whose sister-in-law is left-handed, thus writes to me : "I never heard of any of the rest of the family who were so ; but one of her brothers had much more than the usual facility in using both hands, and in paddling, chopping, etc., used to shift about the implement from one hand to the other in a way which I envied. As to my sister-in-law, she had great advantages from her left-handedness. She was a very good performer on the piano, and her bass was magnificent. If there was a part to be taken only with one hand, she used to take the left as often as the right. But it was at needlework that I watched her with the greatest interest. If she was cutting out, she used to shift the scissors from one hand to the other ; and would have employed the left hand more, were it not that all scissors, as she complained, are made right-handed, and she wished, if possible, to procure a left-handed pair. So also with the needle, she used the right hand generally ; but in many delicate little operations her habit was to shift it to the left hand."

In those and similar cases, the fact is illustrated that the left-handed person is necessarily ambidextrous. He has the exceptional " dexterity " resulting from the special organic aptitude of the left hand, which is only paralleled in those cases of true right-handedness where a corresponding organic aptitude is innate. Education, enforced by the usage of the majority, begets for him the training of the other and less facile hand; while by an unwise neglect the majority of mankind are content to leave the left hand as an untrained and merely supplementary organ. From the days of the seven hundred chosen men of the tribe of Benjamin, the left-handed have been noted for their skill ; and this has been repeatedly manifested by artists. Foremost among such stands Leonardo da Vinci, skilled as musician, painter, and mathematician, and accomplished in all the manly sports of his age. Hans Holbein, Mozzo of Antwerp, Amico Aspertino, and Ludovico Cangiago, were all left-handed, though the two latter are described as working equally well with both hands. In all the fine arts the mastery of both hands is advantageous ; and accordingly the left-handed artist, with his congenital skill and his cultivated dexterity, has the advantage of his right-handed rival, instead of, as is frequently assumed, starting at a disadvantage.

CHAPTER X

IT now remains to consider the source to which the preferential use of the right hand is to be ascribed. The dominant influence of the one cerebral hemisphere in relation to the discharge of nerve force to the opposite side of the body is a fact which is now familiar to the physiologist, and the influence of the left cerebral hemisphere on the action of the right hand has already been alluded to. But this extremely probable source of right-handedness long eluded inquirers, as will be seen from a *résumé* of the various hypotheses suggested by eminent anatomists and physiologists. A very slight consideration of the evidence already adduced in proof of the same prevalent usage from earliest times precludes the idea of its origin in any mere prescribed custom, enforced and developed by education into a nearly universal habit. This becomes the more manifest when it is traced back to primæval races; found incorporated in ancient and modern, savage and civilised languages, and uncontroverted by any evidence calculated to discredit the indications that it was a characteristic of palæolithic and neolithic man.

The inevitable conclusion forced on the inquirer is that the bias in which this predominant law of dexterity originates must be traceable to some specialty of organic structure. On this assumption one feature in the anatomical arrangement of the most important vital organs of the body presents such a diversity in their disposition as would seem to offer a sufficient cause for greater energy in the limbs on one side than on the other, if accompanied by exceptional deviations from the normal condition corresponding to the occurrence of left-handedness; and in this direction a solution has accordingly been sought. The bilateral symmetry of structure, so general in animal life, seems at first sight opposed to any inequality of action in symmetrical organs. But anatomical research reveals the deviation of internal organic structure from such seemingly

balanced symmetry. Moreover, right or left-handedness is not limited to the hand, but partially affects
the lower limbs, as may be seen in football, skating,
in the training of the opera-dancer, etc.; and eminent anatomists and physiologists have affirmed the
existence of a greater development throughout the
whole right side of the body. Sir Charles Bell
says: "The left side is not only the weaker, in
regard to muscular strength, but also in its vital or
constitutional properties. The development of the
organs of action and motion is greatest upon the
right side, as may at any time be ascertained by
measurement, or the testimony of the tailor or shoe-
maker." He adds, indeed, "Certainly this superiority may be said to result from the more frequent
exertion of the right hand; but the peculiarity
extends to the constitution also, and disease attacks
the left extremities more frequently than the right."

With the left-handed, the general vigour and
immunity from disease appear to be transferred to
that side; and this has naturally suggested the
theory of a transposition of the viscera, and the
consequent increase of circulation thereby transferred
from the one side to the other. But the relative
position of the heart is so easily determined in the

living subject, that it is surprising how much force
has been attached to this untenable theory by
eminent anatomists and physiologists. Another
and more generally favoured idea traces to the
reverse development of the great arteries of the
upper limbs a greater flow of blood to the left side;
while a third ascribes the greater muscular vigour
directly to the supply of nervous force dependent
on the early development of the brain on one side
or the other.

So far as either line of argument prevails, it
inevitably leads to the result that the preference of
the right hand is no mere perpetuation of convenient
usage, matured into an acquired, or possibly an
hereditary habit; but that it is, from the first,
traceable to innate physical causes. This, as Sir
Charles Bell conceives, receives confirmation from
the fact already referred to, that right or left-handedness is not restricted to the hand, but affects the
corresponding lower limb, and, as he believes, the
whole side; and so he concludes thus: "On the
whole, the preference of the right hand is not the
effect of habit, but is a natural provision; and is
bestowed for a very obvious purpose." Nevertheless, the argument of Sir Charles Bell is, as a whole,

vague, and scarcely consistent. He speaks indeed of right-handedness as " a natural endowment of the body," and his reasoning is based on this assumption. But much of it would be equally explicable as the result of adaptations following on an acquired habit. Its full force will come under consideration at a later stage. Meanwhile it is desirable to review the various and conflicting opinions advanced by other inquirers.

The theory of Dr. Barclay, the celebrated ana-tomist, is thus set forth by Dr. Buchanan, from notes taken by him when a student : " The veins of the left side of the trunk and of the left inferior extremity cross the aorta to arrive at the vena cava ; and some obstruction to the flow of blood must be produced by the pulsation of that artery." To this Dr. Barclay traced indirectly the preferential use of the right side of the body, and especially of the right hand and foot. " All motions," he stated, " produce obstruction of the circulation ; and ob-struction from this cause must be more frequently produced in the right side than the left, owing to its being more frequently used. But the venous circulation on the left side is retarded by the pulsa-tion of the aorta, and therefore the more frequent motions of the right side were intended to render the circulation of the two sides uniform." The idea, if correctly reported, is a curious one, as it traces right-handedness to the excess of a compensating force for an assumed inferior circulation pertaining naturally to the right side; and incidentally takes into consideration an abnormal modification affecting the development or relative disposition of organs. Both points have been the subject of more extended consideration by subsequent observers. It is curious, indeed, to notice how physiologists and anatomists have shifted their ground, from time to time, in their attempts at a solution of what has been very summarily dismissed by others as a very simple problem; until, as Dr. Struthers remarks, it "has ceased to attract the notice of physiologists only because it has baffled satisfactory explanation."

The eminent anatomist, Professor Gratiolet, turned from the organs in immediate contact with the arm and hand, and sought for the source of right-handedness in another and truer direction, though he failed to realise its full bearings. According to the Professor, in the early stages of fœtal development the anterior and middle lobes of the

brain on the left side are in a more advanced
condition than those on the right side, the balance
being maintained by an opposite condition of the
posterior lobes.   Hence, in consequence of the
well-known decussation of the nerve roots, the right
side of the body,—so far as it is influenced by
brain-force,—will, in early fœtal life, be better
supplied with nervous force than the left side; and
thereby movements of the right arm would precede
and be more perfect than those of the left.   The
bearings of this line of argument in its full com-
pass will come more fitly under review at a later
stage.

Dr. Andrew Buchanan, Professor of Physiology
in the University of Glasgow, in a paper communicated by him to the Philosophical Society of
Glasgow in 1862, entitled "Mechanical Theory of
the predominance of the right hand over the left;
or more generally, of the limbs of the right side
over those of the left side of the body," aimed
at a solution of the question in a new way.
According to him, "the preferential use of the
right hand is not a congenital but an acquired
attribute of man.   It does not exist in the earliest
periods of life."   Nevertheless, "no training could

ever render the left hand of ordinary men equal in strength to the right;" for "it depends upon mechanical laws arising out of the structure of the human body." This theory is thus explained: In infancy and early childhood there is no difference in power between the two sides of the body; but so soon as the child becomes capable of bringing the whole muscular force of the body into play, "he becomes conscious of the superior power of his right side, a power not primarily due to any superior force or development of the muscles of that side, but to a purely mechanical cause. He cannot put forth the full strength of his body without first making a deep inspiration; and by making a deep inspiration, and maintaining afterwards the chest in an expanded state, which is essential to the continuance of his muscular effort, he so alters the mechanical relations of the two sides of his body that the muscles of his right side act with a superior efficacy; and, to render the inequality still greater, the muscles of the left side act with a mechanical disadvantage." Hence the preference for the right side whenever unusual muscular power is required; and with the greater exercise of the muscles of the right side their consequent development follows, until the full predominance of the right side is the result.

This theory is based not merely on the preponderance of the liver and lungs on the right side, but on these further facts: that the right lung is more capacious than the left, having three lobes, while the left has only two; that the liver, the heaviest organ of the body, is on the same side; and that the common centre of gravity of the body shifts, more or less, towards the right, according to the greater or less inspiration of the lungs, and the consequent inclination of the liver resulting from the greater expansion of the right side of the chest.   Herein may possibly lie one predisposing cause leading to a preferential use of the right side.   But the evidence adduced fails to account for what, on such a theory, become normal deviations from the natural action of the body. The position of the liver and the influence of a full inspiration combine, according to Dr. Buchanan, to bring the centre of gravity of the body nearly over the right foot.   Hence in actively overcoming a resistance from above, as when the carter bears up the shaft of his cart on his shoulder, the muscular action originates mainly with the lower limb of the same side, which partakes of the same muscular .power and development as the corresponding upper limb. On all such occasions, where the muscular action is brought directly into play in overcoming the weight or resistance, Dr. Buchanan affirms that the right shoulder is much more powerful than the left, but in the passive bearing of weights it is otherwise. The very fact that the centre of gravity lies on the right side gives a mechanical advantage in the use of the left side in sustaining and carrying burdens; and this assigned pre-eminence of the left side and shoulder, as the bearer of burdens, is accordingly illustrated by means of an engraving, representing " a burden borne on the left shoulder as the summit of the mechanical axis passing along the right lower limb."

In the year following the publication of Dr. Buchanan's *Mechanical Theory*, Dr. John Struthers, Professor of Anatomy in the University of Aberdeen, communicated to the Edinburgh *Medical Journal* a paper, " On the relative weight of the viscera on the two sides of the body, and on the consequent position of the centre of gravity to the right side." In this he shows that the viscera situated on the

right side of the medial line are on an average
22·75 oz. av. heavier than those on the left side.
The right lung, in the male, weighs 24 oz., the left
21, giving a preponderance of 3 oz. in favour of
the right. The average weight of the heart, in the
male, is 11 oz. But the left side is not only the
larger, but the thicker, and as the result of careful
experiments by Dr. Struthers, he assigns to the
right side a full third of the weight of the heart, or
$3\frac{1}{2}$ oz. for the right, and $7\frac{1}{2}$ for the left side. Other
viscera are estimated in like manner, with the result
from the whole that the centre of gravity of the
body, so far as it depends on their weight and
position, is nearly three-tenths of an inch distant
from the medial plane towards the right side. As
a physical agent constantly in operation in the
erect posture, Dr. Struthers states that this cannot
but exert an influence on the attitudes and movements of the body and limbs; and he accordingly
indicates his belief that this deviation of the centre
of gravity furnishes the most probable solution of
the causes "of the preference of the right hand by
all nations of mankind."

The value of Dr. Struthers's determination of
the exact weight and relative eccentricity of the

viscera on the two sides of the body was fully recognised by Dr. Buchanan; and in a communication to the Philosophical Society of Glasgow in 1877 he stated that he had been led to greatly modify his earlier opinions. He had, as shown above, ascribed the predominance of the right hand over the left to the mechanical advantage which the right side has in consequence of the centre of gravity inclining to it. But he says in his later treatise, " I judged hastily when I inferred that this is the ground of preference which prompts the great majority of mankind to use their right limbs rather than their left. The position of the centre of gravity on the right side is common to all men of normal conformation, and furnishes to all of them alike an adequate motive, when they are about to put forth their full strength in the performance of certain actions, to use the limbs of the right side in preference to those of the left. But such actions are of comparatively rare occurrence, and the theory fails to explain why the right limbs, and more especially the right hand, are preferred on so many occasions where no great muscular effort is required; and fails still more signally to explain why some men give a preference to the limbs of the left side, and others manifest no predilection for either." Dr. Buchanan accordingly proceeds to show that there is not only the element of the position of the centre of gravity as the pivot on which all the mechanical relations of the two sides of the body turn; but there is, as he conceives, this other and no less important element. "The centre of gravity situated on the right side is variously placed upwards or downwards, according to the original make or framework of the body." In the great majority of cases this lies above the transverse axis of the body, with a consequent facility for balancing best, and turning most easily and securely on the left foot, with the impulsive power effected by the muscles of the right lower limb. Man is thus, as a rule, right-footed; and, according to Dr. Buchanan, by a necessary consequence becomes right-handed. By a series of diagrams he accordingly shows the assumed variations: (1) the centre of gravity above the transverse axis, with its accompanying right-handedness; (2) the centre of gravity corresponding with the transverse axis, which he assigns to the ambidextrous; and (3) the centre of gravity below the transverse axis begetting left-handedness. The

M

whole phenomena are thus ascribed to the instinctive sense of equilibrium, which constitutes a
nearly infallible guide in all the movements of the
human body.   The greater development of the
organs of motion of the right side is therefore, as
he conceives, not congenital, but arises solely from
the greater use that is made of them.   The relative
position of the centre of gravity depends accordingly
on the original conformation of the body.   Broad
shoulders, muscular arms, a large head and a long
neck, all tend to elevate the centre point; while
the contrary result follows from width at the
haunches and a great development of the lower
limbs.

The intermediate condition, in which the centre
of gravity falls upon the transverse axis, with no
instinctive tendency to call into action the muscles
of the one side of the body in preference to those
of the other, constitutes, according to Dr. Buchanan,
the most happy conformation of the body.   " It
belongs," he says, "more especially to the female
sex.   It is this that so often renders a young girl
a perfect model of grace and agility.   It is the
same conformation that enables the ballet-dancer to
whirl round on her one foot till the spectators are

giddy with looking at her, when she completes her
triumph by revolving with the same ease and
grace on her other foot also." He further adds:
" If accurate statistics could be obtained, I believe
it would be found that while a very great majority
of males are right-handed, the proportion of females
is less; and that, on the contrary, a larger proportion of females than of males are ambidextrous or
left-handed."

Consistently with the ideas thus set forth, both
Dr. Buchanan and Dr. Struthers regard right-
handedness as an acquired habit, though under the
influence and control of the mechanical forces
indicated by them. " As the question," says the
latter, " in so far as it can bear on the cause of the
preference of the right hand, must turn on the
weight and position of the viscera in the child at
the period when the predominance of the right hand
is being gradually developed, in the second and
third years, and afterwards, it is necessary to make
the calculation from the facts as presented in
children." In a letter to myself he thus writes:
" I have again and again verified the fact in my
own children, that in early childhood there is no
preference for one hand more than the other."

But this, as has been already shown, may be partly
due to modes of nursing and other temporary causes
affecting the child in its first infantile stage; and
though it may undoubtedly be affirmed of many,
if not indeed of the majority, of children at that
stage: a certain number will be found to manifest a
distinct preference, at a very early age, for one or
the other hand. In the case of a niece of my own,
the left-handedness showed itself very soon; and
in my grandson it was independently observed by
his mother and nurse, and brought under my notice,
that so soon as he was able to grasp an object and
transfer it from one hand to the other, he gave the
preference to the left hand. A like decided preference for the right hand, though doubtless also
comparatively rare, is more frequent; and the
farther research is carried, the more manifest does
it appear that—whatever be the originating cause,
—the preferential use of what we designate the
right hand is instinctive with a sufficiently large
number to determine the prevalent usage; while
with a smaller number an equally strong impulse
is felt prompting to the use of the left hand, in
defiance of all restraining influences. It is indeed
always necessary to give full weight to the influences

of education, the whole tendency of which, from
early childhood, operates in one direction. The
extent to which this is systematically employed to
develop the use of the one hand at the expense of
the other, is illustrated by the conventional rules
for the use of the knife and fork. It is not
sufficient that the knife shall be invariably held in
the right hand. The child is taught to hold his
knife in the right hand and his fork in the left
when cutting his food; but when either the fork
or spoon is used alone, it must forthwith be transferred to the right hand. All voluntary employment of the left hand in any independent action is
discountenanced as awkwardness or gaucherie; and
thus, with a large majority, especially among the
more refined and conventional classes of society, it is
rendered a comparatively useless member, employed
at best merely to supplement the other.

Reference has already been made to more or less
definite allusions to an exceptional prevalence of
left-handedness in the Punjab, and among the
Sandwich Islanders, the Hottentots, and South
African Bushmen; but they rest apparently on
very partial and limited observations. So far as
appears, it may be confidently assumed that left-

handedness is little more prevalent among the rude
and uncultured classes of society, or among savage
than civilised races; as would certainly be the case
if right-handedness mainly depended on an acquired
habit.   The Rev. George Brown, who has spent
upwards of fourteen years as a missionary among
the Polynesians, informs me that left-handedness is
as rare among the natives of the Pacific Islands as
with ourselves; while in all their languages the
distinction is clearly indicated.   Dr. Rae, whose own
inveterate left-handedness was calculated to draw
his attention to its manifestation among the Indians
and Eskimos with whom he was brought into prolonged contact, only noticed such an amount of ambidextrous facility as is naturally developed in the
paddler, the trapper, and lumberer, in the exigencies
of forest and hunter life.   A similar opinion was
expressed to me by Paul Kane, whose wanderings
as an artist among the tribes of British North
America gave him exceptional facilities for observation; and this conclusion accords with the experience
of members of the Canadian Geological Survey.

Turning next to the idea set forth by Dr.
Buchanan as to the greater preponderance of ambidexterity or left-handedness among females, the

results of my own observation by no means tend to confirm this. I have already noted the case of a lady whose left-handedness is accompanied by great dexterity. I have repeatedly met with cases of ladies who use the needle skilfully with the left hand; but the results of inquiries addressed to musicians and music teachers indicate that in the great majority of cases the cultivation of the left, as the weaker or less skilful hand, has to be sedulously enforced in the training of the female organist and pianist. It is because left-handed pianists are rare that their exceptional dexterity is noted, as in the case of a Canadian lady referred to above: " She had great advantages from her left-handedness. She was a very good performer on the piano, and her bass was magnificent."

Again as to the pirouetting of the trained ballet-dancer, I have been assured that much practice is required to obtain equal facility on either foot. Dr. Buchanan traces the development of the limbs in their active use from the first effort of the child to stand erect; next, the learning to balance itself and turn round on a single foot, and so through a succession of stages, until at length " the child becomes right-footed. It is not till long after that

the right arm acquires its predominance." But
the co-ordination of the right or left hand and the
corresponding foot is by no means so invariable as
to justify any such theory. Hopping, pirouetting,
and standing on one foot are comparatively exceptional actions. The two lower limbs are most
frequently employed in necessarily alternate locomotion. The use of the lower limbs, moreover, is
much more independent of direct conscious volition
than that of the hands, and the purposes to which
their action is applied are rarely of a nature to
invite special attention to them. There is, however,
an instinctive tendency with many, if not indeed
with the majority, to use one foot in preference to
the other, but not necessarily the corresponding one
to the dexterous hand, be it right or left. In skating, for example, where military training has not
habituated to the use of the left foot in starting,
most persons have an instinctive preference for one
foot. So also in football, it is not with most players
a matter of mere chance which foot will be used in
starting the ball. Possibly the same reason may
help to account for the invariable tendency of a
blindfold walker to deviate to one side or the other.
It is scarcely possible to walk in a straight line

with the eyes shut. The one leg apparently tends to outwalk the other. Guided mainly by my own experience, I remarked, when first writing on this subject, that " the same influences appear to affect the whole left side, as shown in hopping, skating, football," etc. But this is partial and uncertain. Dr. Brown-Sequard affirms that right-sidedness affects the arms much more than the legs, and in proof of this he states that " it is exceedingly rare that the leg is affected in the same degree by paralysis as the arm." Dr. Joseph Workman, for many years Medical Superintendent of the Provincial Lunatic Asylum at Toronto, thus writes to me: " When you say that left-footedness is (only) as frequent as left-handedness, I am quite sure you are in error. I remember well, when I was a boy, observing the fact among labouring men engaged in what was called in Ireland ' sodding ' potatoes, in ridges about five feet wide, instead of planting in drills, that in any given number of men, from four up to a dozen, right and left-footedness prevailed about equally. Each pair carrying up the work of a ridge required to be right and left-footed men. I am myself left-footed; and of eight brothers, I believe about four were left and four right-footed.

Sir Charles Bell, in asserting that 'no boy, unless he is left-handed, hops on the left foot,' asserts far more than the fact. I believe every boy will hop on his *spade foot*; at least I do so, and I am not left-handed; and I instinctively do so because I dig with this foot."

Dr. Buchanan states that "in all adults who use the right hand in preference to the left—that is, in the great majority of mankind,—the muscles of the right side, as well as the bones and other organs of motion, are more highly developed than those on the left side;" and the predominance of the upper limb follows, as a rule, the previous development of the lower limb on the same side. The power of overcoming weight or resistance, and that of passively bearing weights, he assigns to opposite sides,—both naturally resulting from the centre of gravity lying on the right side. If such be the case, the great majority of mankind should instinctively use the same side in bearing a burden. A favourable opportunity occurred for testing this question. During a voyage of some days in one of the large steamboats on the Mississippi River, my attention was attracted by the deck-porters, who at every landing are employed in transporting the freight to

and from the levee, and in supplying the vessel with
cordwood.   They constitute, as a class, the rudest
representatives of unskilled labour, including both
whites and negroes.   For hours together they are
to be seen going at a run to and from the lower
deck of the vessel, carrying sacks of grain, bales,
chests, or bundles of cordwood.   Watching them
closely, I observed that some gave the preference to
the right and some to the left shoulder in bearing
their burden ; and this whether, as with bale and
sack, they had it placed on their shoulders by others,
or, as with cordwood, they took the load up themselves.   Noting in separate columns the use of the
right and left shoulder, and in the case of loading
with cordwood the employment of the right and left
hand, I found the difference did not amount to much
more than 60 per cent.   In one case I noted 137
carry the burden on the left shoulder to 81 on the
right; in another case 76 to 45 ; and in the case
of loading cordwood, where the natural action of
the right hand is to place the burden on the left
shoulder, so that the use of the right shoulder
necessarily implies that of the left hand, the
numbers were 65 using the left shoulder and 36
the right.   Here, therefore, a practical test of a very

simple yet reliable kind fails to confirm the idea of
any such mechanical cause inherent in the constitution of the human frame, tending to a uniform
exertion of the right side and the passive employment of the left in muscular action.

While thus questioning some of the assumptions
and deductions set forth by Dr. Buchanan, it must
be acknowledged that his later theory has this great
advantage over other attempts to account for right-
handedness, that it equally meets the cases of
deviation from prevalent usage.   No theory is
worthy of serious consideration which deals with
left-handedness as an exceptional deviation from
habitual action; as where, in his earlier treatise, Dr.
Buchanan expressed the belief that many instances
of left-handedness are "merely cases of ambidextrous-
ness, when the habit of using the left side, in whatever way begun, has given to the muscles of that
side such a degree of development as enables them
to compete with the muscles of the right side, in
spite of the mechanical disadvantages under which
they labour."   "There is an awkwardness," he added,
"in the muscular efforts of such men which seems
to indicate a struggle against nature."   But for those
indisputable cases of "men who unquestionably use

their left limbs with all the facility and efficiency with which other men use their right," he felt compelled either to resort to the gratuitous assumption of "malformations and pathological lesions in early life, diseases of the right lung, contraction of the chest from pleurisy, enlargement of the spleen, distortions of the spine," etc.; or to assume a complete reversal of the whole internal organic structure.

More recently, Dr. Humphry of Cambridge has discussed the cause of the preferential use of the right hand in his monograph on *The Human Foot and Human Hand*, but with no very definite results. Many attempts, he says, have been made to answer the question, Why is man usually right-handed? "but it has never been done quite satisfactorily; and I do not think that a clear and distinct explanation of the fact can be given. There is no anatomical reason for it with which we are acquainted. The only peculiarity that we can discern is a slight difference in the disposition, within the chest, between the blood-vessels which supply the right and left arms. This, however, is quite insufficient to account for the disparity between the two limbs. Moreover, the same disposition is observed in left-handed persons and in some of the lower animals;

and in none of the latter is there that difference
between the two limbs which is so general among
men." Dr. Humphry accordingly inclines to the
view that the superiority of the right hand is not
natural, but acquired. "All men," he says, "are
not right-handed; some are left-handed; some are
ambidextrous; and in all persons, I believe, the left
hand may be trained to as great expertness and
strength as the right. It is so in those who have
been deprived of their right hand in early life; and
most persons can do certain things with the left
hand better than with the right." So far, therefore,
Dr. Humphry's decision would appear to be wholly
in favour of the conclusion that the superiority of
the right hand is an acquired habit. But after
stating thus much, he adds : "Though I think the
superiority of the right hand is acquired, and is a
result of its more frequent use, the tendency to use
it in preference to the left is so universal that it
would seem to be natural. I am driven, therefore,
to the rather nice distinction that, though the
superiority is acquired, the tendency to acquire the
superiority is natural."

This "nice distinction" amounts to something
very like an evasion of the real difficulty, unless

we assume Dr. Humphry to mean only what Dr.
Buchanan states, that during the weakness of infancy
and childhood the two hands are used indiscrimi-
nately; and the preferential use of one side rather
than the other does not manifest itself until the
muscular system has acquired active development.
All the processes by which dexterity in the manipulation and use of tools is manifested, are acquired,
whether the right or the left hand be the one
employed. Men are not born, like ants, bees,
spiders, martins, and beavers, with carpentering,
weaving, modelling, and architectural instincts,
requiring no apprenticeship or culture; though the
aptitude in mastering such arts is greater in some
than in others. If the tendency in their practice
to use the right hand is natural, that is to say,
innate or congenital, then there need be no nice
distinctions in affirming it. But on any clearly
defined physiological deductions of right-handedness
from the disposition of the organs of motion or
circulation, or any other uniform relation of the
internal organs and the great arteries of the upper
limbs, left-handedness becomes mysterious, if not
inexplicable, unless on the assumption of a corresponding reversal of organic structure; for Dr.

Humphry's assertion that "in all persons the left hand may be trained to as great expertness and strength as the right," is contradicted by the experience of left-handed persons in their efforts to apply the same training to the right hand.

To the most superficial observer it is manifest that the anatomical disposition of the vital organs is not symmetrical. The heart lies obliquely, from above downwards, and from right to left; the trachea is on the right side, and the right and left subclavian veins and arteries are diversely arranged. There are also three lobes of the right lung, and only two of the left; and the liver is on the right side. Here, therefore, are sources of difference between the right and left sides of the body, which, if subject to variation, offer a possible explanation of the phenomenon that has so long baffled physiologists. To the variations in the disposition of those organs attention has accordingly been repeatedly directed; as in the occasional origin of the left subclavian artery before the right, which, as hereafter noted, Professor Hyrtl suggested as the cause of the transfer of dexterity to the left limb. But instances have repeatedly occurred of the entire transposition of the viscera. "There are men born," says Dr. Buchanan,

" who may grow up and enjoy perfect health, in
whom the position of all the thoracic and abdominal
viscera is reversed.   There are three lobes of the
left lung and only two of the right; the liver is on
the left side, and the heart is on the right; and so
forth."   Those and other malformations, as well as
pathological lesions, especially if they occur in early
life, may affect the relative power of the two sides;
and Dr. Buchanan at a later date reported a case
that came under his own notice, in which the entire
transposition of the viscera coexisted with left-
handedness.   But he had already adopted the
mechanical theory, subsequently modified, as explained above; and it is only in a closing remark in
his paper of 1862 that he makes a passing reference
to this remarkable coincidence.

Professor Hyrtl of Vienna, the eminent anatomist
already referred to, in discussing the cause of left-
handedness in his *Handbuch der Topographischen
Anatomie* (1860), affirms a correspondence between
the ratio of left-handed persons and the occurrence
of certain deviations from the normal arrangements
of the blood-vessels.   " It happens," he says, " in
the proportion of about two in a hundred cases, that
the left subclavian artery has its origin *before* the

N

right, and in these cases left-handedness exists, as it also often actually does in the case of complete transposition of the internal organs; and it is found that the proportion of left-handed to right-handed persons is also about two to one hundred." Professor Hyrtl thinks that ordinarily the blood is sent into the right subclavian under a greater pressure than into the left, on account of the relative position of these vessels; that in consequence of the greater supply of blood, the muscles are better nourished and stronger; and that therefore the right extremity is more used. In cases of anomalous origin of the left subclavian, etc., the reverse occurs, and therefore the left hand is employed in preference. The theory of Professor Hyrtl has this feature to recommend it, that it assigns a cause for the prevalent habit, which, if confirmed, would equally account for the excep-tional left-handedness; and no proffered solution of the question, founded on organic structure, is deserv-ing of attention which fails to do so. But the statistics of such internal organic structure are not, like those of the transposition of the heart and immediately related organs, accessible in the living subject, unless in very rare exceptions; and the occurrence of one or two cases in which the devia-

tion from the normal arrangement of the artery, or
the entire transposition of the viscera, is found to
coexist with left-handedness, may only be misleading.

A correspondent of *Nature* (9th June 1870)
refers to a case of transposition of the origin of the
right subclavian artery, disclosed by the occurrence
of aneurism, where the person was ascertained to
have been undoubtedly right-handed. In the
following year an interesting article by Dr. Pye-
Smith appeared in the *Guy's Hospital Reports,*
and was subsequently reprinted, with additions,
under the title of " The connection of Left-handedness with transposition of Viscera and other supposed anatomical causes." In this the author
states that he found the deviation from the normal
arrangement of the primary branches of the aorta,
in which the right subclavian arises from the third
part of the aortic arch, to occur four times in 296
dissections. As this variation, he says, " cannot be
recognised during life, its connection with left-
handedness is not easy to investigate. But in one
case, at least, Dr. Peacock ascertained for me that
the subject of this abnormality, whose heart and
arteries he had examined for another purpose, was
right-handed during life." Any one can tell on

which side his heart lies; but the disposition of
the subclavian artery is wholly beyond his cogni-
sance; and, indeed, Professor Hyrtl, while referring
to this abnormal organisation as one probable cause
of left-handedness, does not affirm more than that
the one has been ascertained in some cases to be an
accompaniment of the other. The evidence that in
other cases it has been unaccompanied by left-handedness shows that it is no necessary source of deviation from normal action.

The other theory, that left-handedness is an
inevitable accompaniment of the transposition of
the viscera, is more easily tested. It is one that
has been repeatedly suggested; and has not only
received the sanction of Professor Hyrtl, but is
supported by some undoubted cases in which the
two conditions coexisted. But, as Dr. Pye-Smith
remarks, "a few such instances only prove that
transposition of the viscera does not *prevent* the
subject of the abnormality from being left-handed.
Though attention has hitherto been little drawn to
this point, there are enough cases already recorded
to show that for a person with transposed viscera
to be left-handed is a mere coincidence." In confirmation of this, Dr. Pye-Smith refers to four cases,

one of which came under his own observation in
Guy's Hospital, where the subjects of the abnormal
disposition of the viscera had been right-handed.
In the *Rochester* (N.Y.) *Express* of October 1877
a notice appeared of an autopsy on the body of
George Vail, of Whitby, Ontario, who had recently
died in the Rochester Hospital.   Dr. Stone, as there
stated, "noticed upon the first examination, when
the patient came for treatment, that there was what
is technically called 'juxtaposition of the heart,'
which is a very rare condition.   He was gratified
at the autopsy to have his diagnosis confirmed, the
heart being found on the right side of the body
instead of the left."   I immediately wrote to Whitby,
and in reply was informed that no one had ever
noticed in Vail any indication of his being left-
handed.   A similar case of the transposition of the
viscera, in which, nevertheless, the person was
right-handed, recorded by M. Géry, is quoted in
Cruveillier's *Anatomie* (i. 65).   Another is given
by M. Gachet, in the *Gazette des Hospitaux*, 31st
August 1861; and a third in the *Pathological
Transactions*, Vol. XIX. p. 147 (*Nature*, 28th
April 1870).   This evidence suffices to prove that
there is no true relation between the transposition

of the viscera and left-handedness. Dr. Struthers has shown that "as far as the viscera alone are concerned, the right side is at least $22\frac{3}{4}$ ounces heavier than the left, and that this is reduced $7\frac{3}{4}$ ounces by the influence of the contents of the stomach, leaving a clear preponderance of at least 15 ounces in favour of the right side." The preponderance of the right side, he adds, is probably considerably greater than 15 ounces, and it is rendered still more so in the erect posture. The total weight of viscera on the right side he states at $50\frac{3}{4}$ ounces, while that of the left side is only 28 ounces, giving a visceral preponderance on the right side of $22\frac{3}{4}$ ounces. But if this relative excess of weight on the right side be the true source of right-handedness, the transposition of the viscera ought to be invariably accompanied with a corresponding change. A single example of the preponderant cause, unaccompanied by the assumed effect, is sufficient to discredit the theory.

CHAPTER XI

THERE remains to be considered the source suggested by Professor Gratiolet, when he turned from the organs in immediate contact with the arm and hand to the cerebral centre of nerve force. The statements advanced by him that the anterior convolutions of the left side of the brain are earlier developed than those of the right, when taken in connection with the well-known decussation of the nerve-roots, would account for the earlier development of the muscles and nerves of the right arm; but his opinion has been controverted by competent observers. This, however, does not dispose of the question. The localisation of the mental operations of speaking, naming, and writing in certain specific cerebral centres, and the recognised functional relations of those word-centres with other active cerebration, have given a new significance to the vital action of the brain as the seat of nerve-force. It was only in 1861 that M. Broca definitely assigned the posterior part of the third frontal convolution of the left hemisphere as the seat of articulate speech. More recently this has been followed up by observations suggestive of some possible correlation between the reflex action of the cerebral hemispheres on the limbs; but it has thus far been no more than a passing allusion, tending to beget observation of possible coincidences, such as may be found between left-handedness and either an accompanying transposition of the seat of articulate speech to the right hemisphere, or some prevailing characteristic of the degree of word-memory in the left-handed. A recent observer, Dr. J. Batty Tuke, definitely affirms that "the large proportion of cases of ataxic aphasia occur in association with right-sided hemiplegia, although others are on record in which it has appeared in connection with left-sided hemiplegia in left-handed persons" (*Encyc. Britann.*, art. "Aphasia"). In those an intimate relation is thus established between right or left-handedness and the development of the opposite cerebral hemisphere.

The special limitation of the researches of Dr. Guiseppe of Pisa to "the writing of left-handed persons" naturally directed his attention to this element of cerebration. "Clinical observation and pathological anatomy," he remarks, "have clearly shown that in the foot of the second frontal convolution of the left cerebral hemisphere there is located a centre for the co-ordination and the memory of the movements of writing. The destruction of this centre produces *agraphia*, that is to say, inability to co-ordinate and remember the movements for writing. This graphic centre is situated on the left hemisphere in right-handed persons." At the same time he is careful to assert that both in this writing-centre, and in that of the foot of the third frontal convolution, to which is assigned the co-ordination and memory of the movements for articulate speech : in the case of lesions impairing their powers, it has been found possible to stimulate the corresponding centres of the opposite hemisphere so as in more or less degree to perform their functions ; just as the dormant left hand may be educated to take the place of the paralysed or amputated right hand.

Dr. Guiseppe thus proceeds : " In left-handed persons the centres of the neuro-psychic factors of language are situate in the right hemisphere, as has been shown by well-studied cases. These persons, however, learn to write with the right hand and not with the left. And yet in their right hemisphere there is a potentiality which is very favourable for their education in the co-ordination and the memory of the movements for writing. Left-handed persons perceive that they could learn to write with greater facility with the left hand than with the right ; but education succeeds in awaking and conveniently bringing into action in the left-hand sphere a latent cortical centre, which did not present so favourable a potentiality as that of the right hemisphere. The possibility of investigating what influence in left-handed persons practice with the right hand might develop in the left hemisphere for the explication of language, would certainly constitute a theme for important study" (*Archivio Italiano,* September 1890, pp. 306, 307).

With the attention that is now definitely given to this assignment of the preferential use of one or the other hand to greater or less development of the opposite cerebral hemisphere, renewed observation has been directed to the cerebral source of predominant right-handedness. The discussions in the columns of *Science,* suggested by Professor Baldwin's study of its first manifestations, have revived the reference of it to the assumed excess in development of the left cerebral hemisphere. Dr. T. O'Connor of New York thus reasserts it as an unquestionable though little-known fact: "But it may not be generally known that the left cerebral hemisphere is larger than the right, its inner face (at the great longitudinal fissure) coming very near to the middle line, while the corresponding inner edge of the right hemisphere is well to the right of the median line. The existence, then, of greater nutrition and greater functionating ability in the left hemisphere might well be assumed. But that there is a reason for the greater size, development, etc., of the left hemisphere is evidenced by a study of the conditions of blood-supply to the two hemispheres. The left carotid artery ascends almost perpendicularly, so as to form, as it were, an elongation of the ascending aorta, while the right carotid is given off from the *arteria innominata.* The right vertebral artery is given off by the subclavian after the latter has described its arch and become horizontal, but the left vertebral arises from the apex of the subclavian's curve.   There is thus the distinct advantage to the left hemisphere of a better blood-supply because of the much straighter course taken by the great channels carrying it" (*Science*, 12th December 1890).

This idea of a greater development of the left cerebral hemisphere has been the subject of considerable diversity of opinion.   A marked difference in the weight of the two hemispheres has indeed been repeatedly asserted by well-qualified observers as the result of careful investigation.   M. Broca stated that in forty brains he found the left frontal lobe heavier than the right; and Dr. Boyd, when describing the results obtained by him from observations on upwards of 500 brains of patients in the St. Marylebone Hospital, says : " It is a singular fact, confirmed by the examination of nearly 200 cases at St. Marylebone, in which the hemispheres were weighed separately, that almost invariably the weight of the left exceeded that of the right by at least the eighth of an ounce."   Dr. Brown-Sequard also, as hereafter noted, makes this apparent excess in weight of the left hemisphere of the brain the basis of very comprehensive deductions.   Again Dr. Bastian affirms, as a result of careful observation,

that the specific gravity of the gray matter from the
frontal, parietal, and occipital convolutions respectively is often slightly higher on the left than it is
on the right hemisphere.   The opinion is thus
sustained by some of the most eminent physiologists
who have given special attention to the brain and
its functions.   But, on the other hand, Professor
Wagner and Dr. Thurnam both state that their
careful independent investigations failed to confirm
the results arrived at by M. Broca and Dr. Boyd.
From the weighing of the two hemispheres of
eighteen distinct brains, Professor Wagner found
the right hemisphere the heavier in ten, and the left
in six cases, while in the remaining two they were
of equal weight.   Dr Thurnam, without entering
into details, states that the results of his weighings
did not confirm Dr. Boyd's observations ; adding
that " fresh careful observations are certainly needed
before we can admit the general preponderance of
the left hemisphere over the right."   Though the
two hemispheres of the brain are sufficiently distinct,
they are united at the base ; and even with the
most careful experimenters, the section through the
cerebral peduncles and the corpus callosum is so
delicate an operation that a very slight bias of the

operator's hand may affect the results. That a
difference, however, is occasionally demonstrable in
the weight of the two hemispheres is unquestionable,
and the whole tendency of the most recent investigation is to sustain the hypothesis which refers the
cause of left-handedness to an exceptional excess of
nervous force in the right cerebral hemisphere. But
the results to be anticipated from the partial character of the bias in the majority of the right-handed
would tend to suggest a doubt as to the full
acceptance of the statement of Dr. O'Connor adduced
above. It is rather in accordance with what has
already been affirmed as to the very partial prevalence
of any strongly defined bias in the majority for the
preferential use of either hand, that many brains
should come under the notice of careful observers
where little or no difference can be found between
the two hemispheres. But weight is not the only
element of variation. Dr. Bastian, in *The Brain as
an Organ of Mind*, draws attention to the unsym-
metrical development of the two hemispheres as one
of the most notable peculiarities of the human
cerebrum. This is not only the case with reference
to the number and arrangement of the convolutions,
but it has been noted by various anatomists that the

left hemisphere is very frequently slightly longer than its fellow.

But interesting light has been thrown by patho-logical observations on the comparative relations of the cerebral hemispheres; and in this more than in any other direction we may look for further elucida-tion. As already noted, Sir Charles Bell affirms a general inferiority in muscular strength and in vital properties of the left side of the body, and a greater liability to disease in the left extremities than the right. On the other hand, Dr. O'Connor refers a greater susceptibility to disease of the left hemisphere of the brain to what he assumes as the source of superior vital force. Having assigned the causes of greater development as already cited, he proceeds to affirm that " the greater directness of communication between the heart and left hemisphere explains the greater readiness with which the latter is subjected to certain forms of disease. A clot of fibrine whipped off a diseased valve is carried much more readily because of the direct route (*viâ* the carotid) to the left hemisphere; and in conditions of de-generative weakness of the arteries in general, those of the left hemisphere being subjected to greater pressure in their distal ramifications, will be more apt to yield than corresponding ones in the right."

Dr. Bastian, when commenting in his *Brain as an Organ of Mind* on the specific location of the cerebral function of articulate speech in the third left convolution of the brain, remarks : " It has been thought that a certain more forward condition of development of the left hemisphere—as a result of hereditary right-handedness recurring through generation after generation,—might gradually become sufficient to cause the left hemisphere to take the lead in the production of speech-movements.   Some little evidence exists, though at present it is very small, to show that it is left-handed people more especially who may become aphasic by a lesion of the right third frontal gyrus."   Dr. Bastian further assumes it to be indisputable that the greater preponderance of right-hand movements in ordinary individuals must tend to produce a more complex organisation of the left than of the right hemisphere ; and this both in its sensory and motor regions.   With the left-handed, however, so many motives are constantly at work tending to call the right hand into play, that the compensating influences must in their case tend to check any inequality in the development of the two hemispheres; so that there would seem rather to be a probability in favour of a more equable, and consequently healthful development of both cerebral hemispheres in the left-handed, but really ambidextrous manipulator. But it is to be noted that while Dr. Bastian recognises a correlation between the development of one or other cerebral hemisphere and the greater dexterity of the opposite hand, he is inclined to recognise right or left-handedness as the cause rather than the effect.

Dr. Brown-Sequard, who strongly favours the idea of superiority, both in size and weight, of the left over the right cerebral hemisphere, also ascribes the source of this to the greater frequency and energy of all right-hand movements. He reverts to an argument derived from left-handedness when discussing his theory that the two hemispheres practically constitute two distinct brains, each sufficient in itself for the full performance of nearly all mental operations; though each has also its own special functions, among which is the control over the movements and the organs of opposite sides of the body. "Every organ," he says, "which is put in use for a certain function gets developed, and more apt or ready to perform that function. Indeed, the brain shows this in point of mere size; for the left side of the brain, which is used most, is larger than the right side. The left side of the brain also receives a great deal more blood than the right side, because its action preponderates; and every organ that acts much receives more blood." He accordingly affirms that the growth of the brain up to forty years of age, if not indeed to a considerably later period of life, is sufficiently marked to require the continued enlargement of the hat. The evidence he adduces, based on observing that a hat laid aside for a time and then resumed, always proved to be too small, is probably deceptive. But the growth of the adult brain is no longer disputed. It was indeed affirmed by earlier physiologists, as by Sœmmering, the Wenzels, and Tiedemann, that the brain attained its greatest development not later than seven or eight years of age. But this idea is now entirely abandoned; and—without going so far as to affirm with Dr. Brown-Sequard, who claims that at the age of fifty-seven he found by the test of hat measurement that his head had enlarged within every six months,—the latest observers adduce proof of continuous increase of brain weight, if not of bulk, until the greatest

average weight is reached between thirty and forty
years of age.

On the assumption of Dr. Brown-Sequard that
the left hemisphere of the brain exceeds that of the
right both in size and weight : in the deviations
from this normal condition there ought to be found
the corresponding development of the organ brought
into use.   But, like most other right-handed re-
viewers of the phenomena of left-handedness, he fails
to appreciate the bearings of his own argument in
the case of a left-handed person conforming in many
ways to the usage of the majority, yet instinctively
giving the preference to the left hand.   He dwells
on the fact that very few left-handed persons have
learned to write with the left hand, and that those
who can do not write nearly so well with it as with
the right hand.   Even in persons who are left-
handed naturally, so that the right side of the brain
may be assumed to control the reasoning faculties
and their expression, he argues that the left side of
the brain " can be so educated that the right hand,
which that side of the brain controls, produces a
better handwriting than that by the left hand,
though that is controlled by the better developed
brain."   But the reasoning is alike partial and

misleading. The left-handed person systematically submits to disabilities in his efforts to comply with the usage of the majority, not only in holding his pen in the right hand, but in the direction and slope of the writing. A left-handed race would naturally write from right to left, sloping the letters towards the left, and so would place the right-handed penman at a like disadvantage, wholly independent of any supposed change in the functions or pre-ponderating energy of either hemisphere of the brain. But even in the absence of practice, the command of the left hand in the case of a truly left-handed person is so great that very slight effort is required to enable him to write with ease with that hand.

Reverting once more to the singularly interesting phenomena whereby in certain conditions of cerebral disease, or local injury, the correlation between articulate speech, writing, and even the unconscious expressiveness of gestures, used certain specific con-volutions of the left hemisphere, Dr. Pye-Smith says: "The opinion that some difference between the two sides of the brain has to do with our prefer-ence for the right hand over the left may, perhaps, be supported by two very interesting cases of aphasia occurring in left-handed persons, recorded by Dr. Hughlings Jackson and Dr. John Ogle. In both these patients there was paralysis of the *left* side; so that it seems likely that in these two left-handed people the right half of the brain had the functions, if not the structure, which ordinarily belong to the left. To these cases may be added a very remarkable one published by Dr. Wadham (*St. George's Hospital Report*, 1869). An ambidextrous or partially left-handed lad was attacked with left hemiplegia and loss of speech; he had partly recovered at the time of his death, twelve months later, and then the right insula and adjacent parts were found softened."

The remarkable difference in the convolutions of different brains, and the consequent extent of superficies of some brains over others apparently of the same size, have been matter of special observation, with results lending confirmation to the idea that great development of the convolutions of the brain is the concomitant of a corresponding manifestation of intellectual activity. But the complexity in the arrangement of these convolutions, and the consequent extent of superficies, often differ considerably in the two hemispheres of the same brain. The variations in shape and arrangement of the convolutions in either hemisphere may be no more than the accidental folds of the cerebral mass, in its later development in the chamber of the skull; and within ordinary limits they probably exercise no appreciable influence on physical or mental activity.

In so far as right-handedness is a result of organic structure, and not a mere acquired habit, some trace of it should be found in the lower animals, though in a less degree.   Dr. Buchanan, in discussing his *Mechanical Theory*, notes that, " while the viscera of the quadruped have the same general later-alised position as in man, there is a reason why this should be carried to a greater extent in man than in the quadruped, owing to the much greater lateral development of the chest and abdomen of the human figure, in order to adapt it to the erect posture, as contrasted with the great lateral flattening of the trunk in quadrupeds.   The equipoise is therefore more disturbed in man than in the quadruped." In the case of the monkey, its necessities as a climber no doubt tend to bring all its limbs into constant use; but, possibly, careful study of the habits and gestures of monkeys may disclose, along with their ambidextrous skill, some traces of a preference for the limbs on the one side. The elephant has been repeatedly affirmed to betray a strongly marked right-sidedness; and this is reiterated in a communication by Mr. James Shaw to the Anthropological section of the British Association, where he notes the " curious fact that elephants have been frequently known to use the right tusk more than the left in digging up roots, and in doing other things." But the statement is vague, and, even if confirmed by adequate proof, can scarcely be regarded as the equivalent of right-handedness. In dogs it may be noticed that they rarely move in the direct line of their own body, but incline to one side or the other, the right hind-foot stepping into the print of the left fore-foot, or *vice versâ*. In the horse, as in other quadrupeds, a regular alternation in the pace is manifest, except when modified by education for the requirements of man. I experienced no difficulty in teaching a favourite dog to give the right paw; and no child could more strongly manifest a sense of shame than he did when reproved for the gaucherie of offering the wrong one. The saddle horse is trained to prefer the right foot to lead with in the canter; while the same animal is educated differently when destined for a lady's use;

but I have been informed by two experienced
veterinary surgeons that, while some horses learn
with very slight training to start with the right
foot, others require long and persevering insistency
before they acquire the habit. A curious relation
between man and the lower animals in the manifestation of the organic influences here noted is
indicated by a writer in the *Cornhill Magazine,* when,
referring to the well-ascertained fact that aphasia is
ordinarily accompanied with disease of the right side
of the brain, he says : " Right-sidedness extends to
the lower races.   Birds, and especially parrots, show
right-sidedness.   Dr. W. Ogle has found that few
parrots perch on the left leg.   Now parrots have
that part at least of the faculty of speech which
depends on the memory of successive sounds, and of
the method of reproducing such imitation of them
as a parrot's powers permit ; and it is remarkable
that their left brain receives more blood and is
better developed than the right brain."   The same
writer expresses his doubt as to monkeys showing
any tendency to right-handedness ; but with the
constant use and training of the hands by the
Quadrumana in their arboreal life, opportunities for
the manifestation of any instinctive preference for

either hand must be rare; and is likely to elude all but the most watchful observers.

A paper was communicated by Dr. Delaunay to the Anthropological Society of France, on the subject of right-handedness. I only know of it by an imperfect notice, in which he is reported to look on the preferential use of the right hand as a differentiation arising from natural selection, while he regards ambidexterity as a mere " survival." But Dr. Pye-Smith long ago remarked that " it is clear that in the progress of civilisation one or other hand would come to be selected for the more characteristic human actions for which only one is necessary, such as wielding a pen or other weapon ;" but he recognises the insufficiency of the suggestion, and adds in a footnote : " The difficult point is to guess by what process the right rather than the left hand has been so universally preferred." He then glances at possible guidance to be derived from the study of the habits of savage tribes, though still the old difficulty recurs ; and he thus proceeds : " In default of any better suggestion, might one suggest an hypothesis of the origin of right-handedness from modes of fighting, more by way of illustration than as at all adequate in itself ? If a hundred of our

ambidextrous ancestors made the step in civilisation
of inventing a shield, we may suppose that half
would carry it on the right arm and fight with the
left, the other half on the left and fight with the
right. The latter would certainly, in the long run,
escape mortal wounds better than the former, and
thus a race of men who fought with the right hand
would gradually be developed by a process of natural
selection." The recognition of the shield-hand, and
the passive functions assigned to it, has already
been referred to as one familiar to the ancient Greek
and Roman, and no doubt to other and earlier
nations. But here it is diverted to the service of
one of the latest aspects of evolutionary development, and becomes the begetter instead of the
product of left-handedness. To this idea of right-
handedness as one of the results of a survival of the
fittest, Dr. Delaunay adds the statement, professedly
based on facts which he has accumulated, that
ambidexterity is common among idiots. The results
noted probably amount to no more than the negative
condition of general imbecility, in which the so-called
ambidexterity of the idiot involves, not an exceptional skill in the left hand, equalising it with the
right, but only a succession of feeble and often aim-

less actions manifesting an equal lack of dexterity in either hand. Where left-handedness is strongly developed, it is, on the contrary, not only accompanied with more than average dexterity in the organ thus specialised, but also with a command of the use of the right hand, acquired by education, which gives the individual an advantage over the great majority of right-handed men. The surprise occasionally manifested at any display of dexterity by left-handed performers, as though it were accomplished under unusual disadvantages, is altogether unjustified. In reality, a strongly developed left-handedness is, equally with a strongly developed right-handedness, an indication of exceptional dexterity. Such skill as that of the left-handed slingers of the tribe of Benjamin·is in no way exceptional. All truly left-handed, as well as all truly right-handed persons, are more likely to be *dexterous* than those who are unconscious of any strong impulse to the use of either hand. The bias, whether to the right or the left, is, I feel assured, the result of special organic aptitude. With the majority no well-defined bias betrays any unwonted power, and they merely follow in this, as in so much else, the practice of the pre-dominant number. But there is no such difference

between the two hands as to justify the extent to
which, with the great majority, one is allowed to
become a passive and nearly useless member.   The
left hand ought to be educated from the first no less
than the right, instead of leaving its training to be
effected, imperfectly and with great effort, in later
life, to meet some felt necessity.

Dr. Brown-Sequard, in one of his latest discussions of the closely related, though much more
comprehensive question, "Have we two brains?"
remarks: "We have a great many motor elements
in our brain and our spinal cord which we absolutely
neglect to educate.   Such is the case with the
elements which serve for the movements of the left
hand.   Perhaps fathers and mothers will be more
ready to develop the natural powers of the left
hand of a child, giving it thereby two powerful
hands, if they believe, as I do, that the condition of
the brain and spinal cord would improve if all their
motor and sensitive elements were fully exercised."
Without entering on the discussion of the larger
question of the specific duality of the brain, experience shows that wherever the early and persistent
cultivation of the full use of both hands has been
carried out, the result is greater efficiency, without

any counterbalancing defect. Under no enforcement
of a violation of his innate impulses does the left-
handed person ever exchange hands. He acquires
an educated right hand and retains the dexterity of
the left. In those cases where, by reason of injury
or disease, the sufferer is compelled to resort to the
neglected hand even late in life, it proves quite
possible to train it to sufficient aptitude for all
ordinary requirements. It is therefore obviously
the duty of parents and teachers to encourage the
habitual use of both hands; and in the case of manifest
left-handedness, to content themselves with developing the free use of the right hand without suppress-
ing the innate dexterity of the left. My own experience, as one originally left-handed, is that, in spite
of very persistent efforts on the part of teachers to
suppress all use of the left hand, I am now thoroughly
ambidextrous, though still with the left as the more
dexterous hand. I use the pen in the right hand
but the pencil in the left; so that, were either hand
disabled, the other would be at once available for
all needful operations. Yet at the same time the
experience of a long life assures me that scarcely
any amount of training will suffice to invest the
naturally sinister hand, whether it be the right or

the left, with the dexterity due to innate, congenital,
and therefore ineradicable causes.   Nevertheless we
are bimanous in the best sense, and are meant to
have the free unrestrained use of both hands.   In
certain arts and professions both hands are necessarily called into play.   The skilful surgeon finds
an enormous advantage in being able to transfer his
instrument from one hand to the other.   The dentist
has to multiply instruments to make up for the lack
of such acquired power.   The fencer who can
transfer his weapon to the left hand, places his
adversary at a disadvantage.   The lumberer finds
it indispensable in the operations of his woodcraft
to learn to chop timber right and left-handed ; and
the carpenter may be frequently seen using the saw
and hammer in either hand, and thereby not only
resting his arm, but greatly facilitating his work.
In all the fine arts the mastery of both hands is
advantageous.   The sculptor, the carver, the draftsman, the engraver, and cameo-cutter, each has
recourse at times to the left hand for special manipulative dexterity ; the pianist depends little less on
the left hand than the right ; and as for the organist,
with the numerous pedals and stops of the modern
grand organ, a quadrumanous musician would still

find reason to envy the ampler scope which a Briareus could command. On the other hand, it is no less true that, while the experience of every thoroughly left-handed person shows the possibility of training both hands to a capacity for responding to the mind with promptness and skill: at the same time it is apparent that in cases of true left-handedness there is an organic specialisation which no enforced habit can wholly supersede.

Having determinately arrived at the conclusion that the source of right-handedness, and so of the exceptional occurrence of left-handedness, is to be sought for in the preponderant development of one or other hemisphere of the brain, and that, therefore, the test has to be sought in the examination of the brains of persons of exceptional dexterity, whether in the use of their right or left hand, the difficulty has been to obtain the desired objects of study. A considerable number of observations are desirable ; and those can only be gradually accumulated as opportunities present themselves to observant students. As already noted, men of the first eminence have differed on the question of the greater weight of the left than of the right cerebral hemisphere ; nor does a study of the ordinary manifesta-

tions of right-handedness encourage us to expect a
very marked difference in the cerebral hemispheres
in the majority of men.   It need not therefore
surprise us to find so able and experienced an
observer as Dr. Thurnam reviewing the data published by Boyd, Brown-Sequard, and Broca, and
expressing as his final conviction that further careful
observations are needed before the general preponderance of the left hemisphere over the right can be
accepted as an established truth.

As already noted, Dr. Boyd gives as the result
of his observations on upwards of 500 human
brains, that the weight of the left hemisphere
almost invariably proved to be in excess of that
of the right.   In forty cases Dr. Broca found similar
results, and observers of less note confirm them ; so
that but for the eminent authorities by whom those
conclusions have been challenged, it would seem
presumptuous to refuse them acceptance.   But,
countenanced by this conflict of opinion, it may
be permissible to review the question in the
narrower aspect of the present inquiry.   Testing
it then by a reverse process, and assuming hypo-
thetically that the exceptionally dexterous right-
handed man will be found to have the left hemi-

sphere the heavier, and the true left-handed man
vice versâ, the results arrived at by Dr. Boyd are
altogether in excess of what might be anticipated.
The number of the exceptionally dexterous right-
handed, with an invincible instinctive preference
for the use of that hand, though large in comparison
with the no less dexterous left-handed, are nevertheless a minority. Habit, social usage, and education in all its forms, in the school, the drawing-
room, the workshop, in all the arts of peace, and
in nearly every operation of war, have so persistently
fostered the development of the favourite hand that
it is scarcely possible to arrive at any reliable
statistics in proof of the initial proclivities of the
large majority of conformists. Only a prolonged
series of observations such as those already noted
by Professor Baldwin, made at the first stage of
life, and based on the voluntary and the un-
prompted actions of the child, can supply the
needful data. But the careful observations of many
years, prompted by a desire to master the source
of an exceptional instinctive habit, have convinced
me that the bias towards the preferential use of
either hand in many, probably in the majority of
cases, is slight. It is sufficient to lead to their follow-

ing the practice of the determinately right-handed majority, but would not in itself present an obstacle to conformity to any prevalent usage, or to the influence of education.   If then the preference of either hand furnishes any index of the relative development of the two cerebral hemispheres, what we may reasonably look for is a certain considerable percentage of brains with the weight of the left hemisphere in excess; a small percentage equally definitely characterised by the preponderance in the right hemisphere; while in the average brain the difference will be so slight as to be apt to escape observation.   It is further to be noted that if the habitual use of the right hand tends in any degree to stimulate the development of the left cerebral hemisphere, then the examples of strongly-marked cases of such must greatly exceed those of the reverse type; since the left-handed man is almost invariably ambidextrous, and so subjects both hemispheres to the frequent stimulus of efferent nerve-force.

If the attention of physiologists devoted to cerebral investigations is specially turned to the present aspect of research, cases of well-marked left-handed patients, or what is manifestly of even greater significance, of exceptionally dexterous right-handed patients, in hospitals, asylums, and gaols, will from time to time present themselves. It has indeed been affirmed that left-handedness prevails among the "light-fingered" experts who find frequent lodging in our gaols. The statement rests on no basis of statistical evidence; but I can readily imagine that a left-handed pickpocket turning his exceptional dexterity to account, might find at times the same advantage that Ehud, the son of Gera the Benjamite, derived from using the hand ordinarily recognised as passive or inert. As to the more daring burglar, his sinister dexterity fills peaceful householders with trepidation as soon as the rumour transpires of his presence in their midst. In reality, however, the fancied prevalence of left-handedness among savages, criminals, and idiots, is a mere reflex of the long prevalent misconception that the preferential use of the left hand is solely due to acquired habit, incurable awkwardness, and incapacity. This is an idea that has often checked the development of exceptional dexterity and a full command of both hands.

Meanwhile it is only in so far as the hand may prove to be an index of the brain that observation

is possible on the living subject.   If the transposition
of the viscera, and the exceptional pressure of the heart
on the right, instead of the left side, were the source
or the unvarying concomitant of left-handedness
this could be tested with ease on the living subject.
But the brain is beyond our reach; though pathological phenomena, along with the results of vivisection in the study of lower animal life, have thrown
a flood of light on its functions; as well as on the
localisation of specific cerebrations in their relation
to sense, to language, and to general perceptions as
elements of mental action.

A monograph on left-handedness, ultimately
printed in the *Proceedings of the Royal Society of
Canada for* 1886, was long delayed, in the hope of
meeting with some response to appeals I had repeatedly addressed to medical friends, in the expectation that, sooner or later, some strongly-marked case
of left-handedness among hospital or other patients
might afford an opportunity for securing an autopsy
of the brain.   But unless the fact has been previously
noted, there is little occasion in the passive condition
of mortal disease to give prominence to the left-
handed action of a patient, and I had to rest content
with inviting attention to the subject when a

favouring opportunity presented itself. But my anticipations of the result to be looked for were very definite, could the required organ of exceptionally developed nerve-force be got hold of. There was indeed one very suitable brain close at hand, and available for many curious speculative researches; but wholly beyond reach of ocular investigation by me. I could therefore only draw attention to it as possibly accessible to some future investigator, since even vivisection must needs defeat my aim. I accordingly remarked : " My own brain has now been in use for more than the full allotted term of threescore years and ten, and the time cannot be far distant when I shall be done with it. When that time comes, I should be glad if it were turned to account for the little further service of settling this physiological puzzle. If my ideas are correct, I anticipate as the result of its examination that the right hemisphere will not only be found to be heavier than the left, but that it will probably be marked by a noticeable difference in the number and arrangements of the convolutions."

Happily since then the long-coveted opportunity has been afforded me. In February 1887 I learned from Dr. Daniel Clark, Superintendent of

the Provincial Asylum at Toronto, of the death of
Thomas Neilly, a patient who had been under the
doctor's care for nearly two years. He was a
native of Ireland, had served in the army, and was
there noted as so inveterately left-handed that he
was placed on the extreme left of his company, and
allowed the exceptional usage of firing from the left
shoulder. He could read and write, and was considered a man of good intelligence, till he attained
his thirty-fourth year, when symptoms of insanity
manifested themselves, and he was removed to the
asylum, where he died. My colleague, Professor
Ramsay Wright, accompanied me to the asylum on
my learning of his death. The brain was removed
and the two hemispheres carefully weighed. Cerebral
disease manifested itself in the evidence of softening
of the brain. But it was fully available for the
special inquiry; and the result of the testing experiment was to place beyond doubt the preponderant
weight of the right cerebral hemisphere. No comprehensive inductions can be based on a single case,
but its confirmatory value is unmistakable at this
stage of the inquiry; and thus far it sustains the
conclusions previously arrived at, and justifies the
assignment of the source of left-handedness to an

exceptional development of the right hemisphere of the brain; with results of a greatly more comprehensive character, apparently affecting the whole functions ordinarily located in the opposite cerebral hemisphere.

THE END

Printed by R. & R. CLARK, *Edinburgh.*

For EU product safety concerns, contact us at Calle de José Abascal, 56–1°, 28003 Madrid, Spain or eugpsr@cambridge.org.

www.ingramcontent.com/pod-product-compliance
Ingram Content Group UK Ltd.
Pitfield, Milton Keynes, MK11 3LW, UK
UKHW010337140625
459647UK00010B/652